Additional Praise for *Effective Social Learning: A Collaborative, Globally-Networked Pedagogy*

"When this book first came to my attention, I was halfway through a one-month professional development program that my (Canadian) university is delivering in China for a group of professors from Chinese universities. It would have been really useful if I had seen it before I left Canada. I'm sure it will be a major resource the next time we deliver the program here. Our program depends entirely on intercultural collaboration, and the many insights into such collaborations will help us to improve both the face-to-face and online aspects of our program."

Walter Archer
University of Alberta

"Loewen, Lester, and Duncanson-Hales sketch how internet-based technology can successfully be put to practical use in our physical classrooms. Through illustrations of multiple victories and pitfalls, the team provides a large set of tools for navigating social learning environments. *Effective Social Learning* is essential reading for those interested in generating networked collaboration between student peers and scholars across international learning spaces."

Kristian Petersen
University of Nebraska–Omaha

"A highly informed, accessible, and practical guide for teachers keen to develop cross-cultural, innovative, engaged learning opportunities for their students. *Effective Social Learning* is prepared by experienced teachers who model transparency, collaborative teaching, and generosity of spirit."

Michel Desjardins
Wilfrid Laurier University

Effective Social Learning
A Collaborative, Globally-Networked Pedagogy

Nathan Loewen

with

Christopher Duncanson-Hales
G. Brooke Lester

EFFECTIVE SOCIAL LEARNING
A Collaborative, Globally-Networked Pedagogy

Copyright © 2014 Fortress Press. All rights reserved. Except for brief quotations in critical articles or reviews, no part of this book may be reproduced in any manner without prior written permission from the publisher. Visit http://www.augsburgfortress.org/copyrights/ or write to Permissions, Augsburg Fortress, Box 1209, Minneapolis, MN 55440.

Cover image: © denphumi/iStock/Thinkstock
Cover design: Laurie Ingram
Book design: PerfecType, Nashville, TN

Library of Congress Cataloging-in-Publication Data is available
Print ISBN: 978-1-4514-8876-0
eBook ISBN: 978-1-4514-8952-1

The paper used in this publication meets the minimum requirements of American National Standard for Information Sciences — Permanence of Paper for Printed Library Materials, ANSI Z329.48-1984.

Manufactured in the U.S.A.

Contents

Acknowledgments vii

1 The Approach
Nathan Loewen 1

Extend the Innovation 1.1—G. Brooke Lester 4
Extend the Innovation 1.2—G. Brooke Lester 8
Extend the Innovation 1.3—Christopher J. Duncanson-Hales 9
Chapter Response I: How Did We Get to Here?—G. Brooke Lester 20
Chapter Response II: Finding Your "Plan B": Asynchronous and
  Synchronous Technology—Christopher J. Duncanson-Hales 23

2 The Collaboration
Nathan Loewen 25

Extend the Innovation 2.1—G. Brooke Lester 27
Extend the Innovation 2.2—Christopher J. Duncanson-Hales 30
Extend the Innovation 2.3—G. Brooke Lester 38
Chapter Response I: Facilitating Virtual Community—G. Brooke Lester ... 42
Chapter Response II: Finding the Courage
  to Teach Dialogically—Christopher J. Duncanson-Hales 45

3 The Foundation
Nathan Loewen 47

Extend the Innovation 3.1—G. Brooke Lester 51
Extend the Innovation 3.2—G. Brooke Lester 58
Extend the Innovation 3.3—Christopher J. Duncanson-Hales 60
Chapter Response I: Preparing for a Cross-Cultural
  Classroom Experience—G. Brooke Lester 62

Chapter Response II: Considering Learning Disabilities in
Collaborative Learning Environments—*Christopher J. Duncanson-Hales* 66

4 The Content
Nathan Loewen 73

Extend the Innovation 4.1—G. Brooke Lester 78
Extend the Innovation 4.2—G. Brooke Lester 82

Chapter Response I: Teaching Online: The Bad News, the Worse News, and What to Do about It—*G. Brooke Lester* 90

Chapter Response II: International Experiential Learning—
Christopher J. Duncanson-Hales 92

5 The Plan
Nathan Loewen 99

Extend the Innovation 5.1—G. Brooke Lester 104
Extend the Innovation 5.2—Christopher J. Duncanson-Hales 108
Extend the Innovation 5.3—G. Brooke Lester 115

Chapter Response I: Assign "Fails" to Find Digital Learning Wins—
G. Brooke Lester 117

Chapter Response II: Minding the Divides—*Christopher J. Duncanson-Hales* 119

6 The Details
Nathan Loewen 125

Extend the Innovation 6.1—G. Brooke Lester 131
Extend the Innovation 6.2—G. Brooke Lester 139

Chapter Response I: Creating a Community of Practice—*G. Brooke Lester* 145

Chapter Response II: Creating Communities of Scholars—
Christopher J. Duncanson-Hales 147

Selected Bibliography 149

Acknowledgments

The book in your hands was written while I was a visiting scholar at the University of Alabama's Center for Instructional Technology, thanks to the initiative of Christina Frantom and the support of Ivon Foster. The inspiration for this book begins within Vanier College and CÉGEP de Sept-Îles, both of which are a part of the CÉGEP system within Quebec, Canada (Collège d'enseignment général et professionnel). Sophie Jacmin and Sharon Coyle began "Project J@nus," and invited me to participate in their experiments with collaborative online learning. Sharon is the best colleague with whom I could imagine doing collaborative team teaching. The technical ingenuity of Jocelyn Trudeau and Dennis Lafontaine at Vanier and Jean-Pierre Poirlier at Sept-Îles enabled them to get started, and these fabulous IT technicians continued their energetic support when I took responsibility for the project. Eric Lozowy, the Dean of Sciences and General Studies at Vanier College, gave instrumental support and administrative insight to transform the project into what is now the Virtual Team Teaching Network. I met my two most important conversation partners for the contents of this book at Eric's suggestion. Jennifer Mitchell skillfully brings a frank and practical pedagogical sensibility to every conversation. Vanier is so lucky to have her as their education technology pedagogical counselor. Through her pedagogical acumen, Isabelle Delisle helped me understand how the principles guiding online learning at CÉGEPaDistance could be applied to collaborative online learning. The financial support for our shared projects and the creation of the Network is due to the support from the Canada-Quebec Entente.

I have done collaborative networked teaching with many teachers over the last six years, but André Alizzi (CÉGEP de Sept-Îles) stands out. Teaching with him is always enjoyable and, although he and I have only interactive virtually, I count him among my good friends. Every teacher who has interacted with me deserves a mention, as I am honored to have them transform my understandings of teaching and learning thus far: Stacey DeWolfe, Marianne Lynch, Caroline Chwojka, Stéphane Giroux, Sevak Manjikian, Maggie Kathwaroon, Lili Petrovic, Jacky Vallée, Matthieu Sossoyan, Gwendolyn Guth, Stacie Sivyer, Lon Appleby, Martin Brière, Mario Corbin, and Irina Gogoleva. Gordon Aronoff, my office mate and best friend at Vanier, showed gracious forebearance as I hosted one Skype conversation after another in between classes. I also wish to thank those who helped my classrooms go global. They are all establishing themselves as world-changing and world-class scholars, and it was my honor for them to virtually teach with me in my classrooms: Daria Gage, David Tshimba, Raihana Kamal, Sandra Rios, Antoinette Davis, Sarbeswar Sahoo, Melanie Hadida, Shivani Bothra, Thien-Huong T. Ninh, Renny Thomas, Mustaghfiroh Rahayu, Sertaç Sehlikoglu, and Justyna Nicinska.

Special thanks goes to David Schoenknecht at Fortress Press. I was inspired by the short conversation we had during at a Wabash Center event during the 2012 meeting of the American Academy of Religion. I was glad, then, when he contacted me to begin working on an innovative online textbook project the following year. I am impressed by his vision and his ability to lead cutting-edge collaborative projects. I have thoroughly enjoyed working with my collaborators on this text, Christopher J. Duncanson-Hales and G. Brooke Lester.

Finally, I must acknowledge the joy and energy of living with Merinda Simmons. I find myself smiling everywhere I go because of her. The arrival of Arlo in our lives punctuates that exhilaration with a thousand laughs.

Chapter 1

The Approach

Nathan Loewen

At a Glance

In this chapter you will be introduced to Collaborative Networked Teaching and Learning.

- Introduction
- What is collaborative networked teaching and learning?
- Ending teacher isolation through collaboration
- Why should I do this?
- A history of collaborative networked teaching and learning
- The three pillars of effective social learning

Introduction

A Snapshot

Two teachers meet at a seminar on intercultural learning. This is no joke, but there is a punchline. One teacher is from Montreal, and the other from Moscow. Both teach on the topic of religious studies in their respective institutions, and both wish to find ways and means to enrich their classrooms. Within minutes, they hatch a

---

*QR code URL: http://www.ascd.org/ASCD/pdf/journals/ed_lead/el_198602_lieberman2.pdf.

plan: they will connect their classrooms in real time using Skype to discuss common themes in their courses. During lunch, they have a casual conversation about their research interests and goals for teaching. Business cards are exchanged and the teachers return to their home countries.

A month later, they exchange emails and agree for a personal Skype meeting, during which they agree upon the basic parameters: the session will take place during Montreal's early morning and Moscow's late afternoon, the language will be English, and some sort of discussion will take place between their classrooms. After considering several topics, the teachers switch to considering goals: What do they both want their classes to *do*? Well, they both wish to teach their students how to extract an argument from a philosophical text and form a counterargument to that position. A class session plan emerges from their discussion, and they agree to work on the session plan by creating documents (the teachers' plan and class instructions) on Google Drive. Learners will be asked to prepare three-hundred-word statements on their opinions about the afterlife. These statements will be circulated between the classes prior to the actual session. Individuals will be asked to respond to each other over the class-to-class Skype connection.

On the day of the class session, the classrooms filled quickly. The homework preparations had already created excitement for both classes. In Montreal, there was amazement at the complexity of the Moscow arguments. In Moscow, there was fascination with the diversity of perspectives and speculation. The teachers began the session by acknowledging each other first and saying a few words about themselves. The teachers then introduced their classes to each other with a simple, collective wave and "Hello!"

The teachers reviewed the activity using the same document that they had earlier co-created on Google Drive and circulated to their classes. The exchanges then ensued, with the teachers calling upon the prearranged sets of pairs. Not everyone would have a chance to engage with his or her partner, due to limited time, but everyone would have the opportunity to observe the live exchange of thoughts and ideas from one continent to another. The class session had its share of surprised expressions, questions for clarification, awkward silences, and moments of brilliance. When it was all done, the teachers closed the session with another collective wave and "Goodbye!" (See chapter 5 for a detailed illustration.)

Where Effective Social Learning Begins

I do not know how to begin this book without referring to the Internet. I wanted to start by writing about the amazing amount of discussion going on in higher education on the topic of innovation in teaching and learning. And I wanted to remark how this is particularly the case where technology is concerned. I then thought about how I might ask you, the reader, to substantiate this claim. I began typing on my laptop—and not writing, mind you—that just a few minutes of Internet browsing would net solid results on Websites such as The Chronicle of Higher Education, Edutopia, the "education" page on SmartBrief, Edudemic, or the *New York Times* Higher Education page. These are among my usual suspects on my "hit list" when I wish to learn about new ideas and trends for the practice of teaching and learning.

The Approach   3

While it is pedestrian to remark about the ubiquity of the Internet and Web-based applications, the point is worth repeating. "Web 2.0" is the name for the emergence of socially interactive applications that work on technological platforms with inputs and outputs beyond the typical screen-and-keypad interface. Cameras and microphones now appear on almost every new Internet-capable device, and users of these devices find it increasingly natural to use these interfaces. My father, who recently retired, never used a computer at his workplace. But he has no qualms about seeing his grandchildren in real time. We live over one thousand miles apart!

This book is focused on how educators and learners may start moving beyond the screen and keypad in education. If you are reading this book, you are likely already familiar with the use of email as well as some kind of messaging within a "learning management system" (LMS) such as Moodle, Blackboard, Desire2Learn, Canvas, and the like. Your experience with the latter may already include other interactions beyond email and messaging, but they are essentially the same thing. Text is being created and read by someone else, such as turning in an essay online, contributing to a wiki, posting on a forum, or keeping a class blog. These kinds of communication are "asynchronous," which means they can happen at different times. Even social media and MOOCs (massive open online courses; see below) retain this conventionally asynchronous interaction. Ultimately, those necessary gaps in time make these uses of the Internet and Web no different than letter writing. This book aims to help you leverage today's technology to take teaching and learning beyond glorified pen-pal interactions.

And herein lies the challenge or problem this book addresses: If today's technology allows for a level of social interaction never before imaginable, how do we teach in a way that takes advantage of this? The answer that I propose to you is to do collaborative networked teaching and learning. Throughout every chapter, I will explore and explain how to establish an inter-institutional teaching partnership that will promote dialogue amongst geographically separated classrooms in real time. By my lights, this is where effective social learning really begins.

 John Seely Brown, who calls himself "the Chief of Confusion," gave an address to the U.S. Department of Education summit on "Reimagining Education: Empowering Learners in a Connected World."[1]

What Is Collaborative Networked Teaching and Learning?

This book proposes to take your institution's existing Internet-based technology, which is already useable and accessible, to create applied learning experiences.

---

1. QR code URL: http://www.c-span.org/video/?312978-1/us-education-strategy-digital-world.

My running assumption throughout the book is that your objective—whether you are on a full-time contract or doing part-time or adjunct work—is to teach real students in real time in an actual bricks-and-mortar classroom. Everything in this book is written from this standpoint. My assumption is that your teaching does not involve a distance-based element where learners are geographically separated monads in the ethersphere. The approach to teaching and learning in this book is meant to put the best of the bricks-and-mortar classroom in touch with the best opportunities afforded by the Internet.

Sidebars throughout the book called "Extend the Innovation" invite you to explore ideas related to integrating collaborative networked learning into your existing pedagogy.

Extend the Innovation 1.1

G. Brooke Lester

Of course, your current teaching *may indeed* involve a distance-based element where learners are geographically separated monads in the ethersphere.

An early revelation to me as a networked instructor was that synchronous teaching is harder than asynchronous teaching, a fact counterintuitive to most of us since we've been teaching synchronously for years in our nonnetworked brick-and-mortar classrooms. All of our preparation and experience is in service to synchronous learning. Lots of things about teaching are hard, but synchrony? To paraphrase Jay-Z, "I got 99 problems, but synchrony ain't one."

That is, until we begin networked learning—in any form. My first networked course was a fully online class that included a weekly synchronous hour, mediated by means of a "virtual classroom" to which students logged on individually from their own computers. And, guess what? That was the hardest hour to use well. Lecture wastes that synchronous moment, and collaboration requires not only informed planning but a generous helping of luck (between students falling offline, forgetting headsets and generating echoes, and navigating etiquette toward efficiency).

Like many instructors, I've arranged my online-instructor professional development around asynchrony and a one-to-many structure, with (if I don't say so myself) often excellent results, largely through the example of amazing forerunners and through forbearance of creative learners. Now, Nathan Loewen invites me (and you, distant-element monad-teacher) to enlarge our toolkit again and revisit the possibilities of the classroom-to-classroom synchronous experience.

The most basic form of collaborative networked teaching and learning is a live (i.e., synchronous) video session that engages two classrooms with a session plan. This basic form can be easily accentuated in order to integrate more clearly this learning experience into each teacher's curriculum. For example, preparatory materials and instructions can be circulated—asynchronously—using open and free online tools (e.g., a blogging site, cloud-based file storage, or an open LMS like Moodle). These same tools can be used to encourage continued interaction among the learners for the creation of shared products that demonstrate how they have achieved the goals and objectives set out by the collaborating teachers. For example, learners can continue to work in real time with each other by way of live applications for video, audio, or chatting. They can use these to assist their creation of shared projects in real time to create Web-based documents, images, and videos. Later collaborative networked teaching and learning might involve sessions where the two groups of students present or evaluate projects with each other.

In principle, collaborative networked teaching and learning involves the creation of real-time learning experiences that employ an active learning pedagogy. In every aspect of the basic scenarios described above, the emphasis is on *synchrony*. The point is not to create a pen-pal learning task, akin to homework or an in-class assignment, but a real-time learning experience. Learners will be confronted with the challenge to communicate effectively, and they will need to engage that challenge actively during the class session. The emphasis on synchronous sessions introduces a certain kind of contextual learning. The added "context" is unconventional. It is the dynamics of communicating in real time with others who are not physically present in the classroom. That dynamic heightens the importance of effective communication. This unique context, unlike a pen-pal series of exchanges, can either serve to enrich conventional teaching or to reorient conventional teaching around these dynamic learning experiences.

Here is another way of describing collaborative networked teaching and learning. Imagine two classrooms that are side by side in your institution's hallway. Have you ever taught in this situation? Have you ever heard another teacher or the students inside another class while yours is in session? Now, imagine a hole—or several holes—being punched between these two rooms. All of a sudden, you would be able to communicate with another teacher and group of students. It would make sense either to cover the holes and teach in complete silence or to begin collaborating with the other teacher. Collaborative networked teaching and learning embraces the latter option, and sets out to knock holes into virtual walls with Web-based tools to merge two geographically separated groups of learners.

In my opinion, these sorts of sessions provide the most dynamic form of social learning possible with today's technologies. As with all teaching and learning, the effectiveness of these sessions depends greatly upon a teacher's dedication to a reflective teaching practice. That said, however, effective social learning using collaborations across networks requires transparency and communication. This is necessary for the collaborating teachers, their institutional context, and for their learners. The existence of free and open Web-based platforms creates transparency and enables communication between the teachers as well as among *all* the students involved. The loss of transparency greatly risks a breakdown of communication and an unsuccessful collaboration.

Ending Teacher Isolation through Collaboration

Virtual Teams: From Business to Education

Collaborative networked teaching and learning partly draws upon local innovation as well as recent trends in the world of private business. Teaching and learning in business schools have long used collaborative sessions because so much of what happens during employment is team based. Graduates from MBA programs, for example, will likely find themselves working or leading a team. As a result, a thorough knowledge of collaboration is a necessity for their future success.

Today's technology adds a further dimension that is increasingly at the heart of contemporary business. Collaborations and teamwork are increasingly distributed across the dimensions of space, time, and organizational structures. Teams may be working within a localized region, or they might be working on the same project while in different locations around the planet. The membership of these teams might be socially homogenous. More often than not, however, geographically distanced collaborations are increasingly taking place across social and cultural differences. These differences can exist within an organization, or they might be cross-organizational collaborations. Nothing about this is absolutely new; after all, it took a Japanese company (Sony) and one in the Netherlands (Philips) to create the compact-disc format and technology that was introduced in 1982!

Collaborative networked teaching and learning draws on the idea of the virtual team. Any virtual team consists of three or more persons who work together to accomplish a shared objective through an organized set of goals and activities despite—or because of!—their dispersion across locations. Virtual teams allow businesses to act with agility and address several local situations while accomplishing a broader goal that encompasses several contexts. And while this demands greater investments in terms of trust building and team building in the form of greater amounts of communication frequency and attention to communication quality, the levels of reliability and pan-organizational dispersal of skills and knowledge create a greatly enriched human-resource asset. From an educational perspective, the implementation of virtual teams into teaching and learning makes the same input demands with the result of deeper learning on the part of those who complete the course or move on from that institution.

Collaborative Networked Philosophy: The Host-Guest/Guest-Host

The concerns and interests of private business do not translate to educational scenarios in their entirety. I am presenting collaborative networked teaching and learning as something that takes place inter-institutionally. In particular, I think this approach can work very well in smaller institutions of under five thousand students. However, I can imagine that this approach might work well with larger institutions that have dispersed campus networks or extension campuses. I think that social learning is most effective when practiced on an inter-institutional level. When the collaboration happens among networked institutions, there is a greater demand for transparency along with attention to the frequency and clarity of communications. Transparency removes the guesswork from relationships because it entails being frank and open about everyone's motives, goals, and intentions—both in the short and longer terms. Frequent communications are not so much a call for "noisy chatter" but, rather, everyone involved agreeing to update each other on all developments. This is particularly the case if communications are polite without being wordy and pointed without being terse. Noisy and redundant communications are actually reduced when, for example, teachers copy each other on their communications with their respective IT teams and administrators. These communications prevent imaginations from running wild in the midst of "radio silence." Only when it is really the case that nothing at all is happening should partners get the impression that nothing is happening. The demand for these key traits quickly becomes apparent for relationships within the individual institutions as well as between them—and even more so when these partnerships take place on an international level.

As a pedagogical approach, collaborative networked teaching relies upon reciprocity. Elsewhere in the book, this will be discussed in terms of hospitality. The main point here is that cross-institutional collaborations require a great level of back-and-forth. As an educational experience and a resource for professional development, these collaborations require a "double hosting" situation. Externally speaking, each teacher and classroom—indeed, each institution—plays host to the other. Each plays guest to the other, too. Internally speaking, a greater level of interaction is required among teachers, professionals, technicians, and administrators who need greater transparency and communication to make possible effective social learning in a collaborative networked learning session. Using the Internet's free and open Web-based tools provides a neutral space in which this host–guest/guest–host collaboration may be most effectively actualized.

Moving Away from Isolation toward the Future of Education

Adapting the virtual-team approach to education makes sense to me because I have a difficult time seeing how the future could be anything less than social. The distribution of social-friendly devices is increasing, where simple and reliable tools are also fairly affordable. The resulting diffusion makes it easy for me to imagine how teachers and learners can see themselves using applications for real-time interactions. The Internet is becoming more widely available around the world, too; and this is accompanied by a correlative increase in the potential for intercultural and regional awareness. I think it should be entirely possible to imagine teaching and learning that reflects the social dynamics that accompany these contextual changes.

To see collaborative networked learning as integral to teaching is something that I hope this book is able to present in a convincing way. The opening of your classroom to that of another teacher and other learners should be an exciting possibility.

I think that a correlative trend can then be started, where teachers and learners alike cease to see their courses as isolated or shut off from the outside world. Pedagogically speaking, however, I do not think that this entails opening the classroom onto a wide, massively open domain. I leave this to the MOOC enthusiasts. Instead, I think that the focus allowed by a relative isolation of the classroom enables a much more clear emphasis on collaboration. In these situations, learning involves the negotiation of meaning and teachers may enable learners to participate in focused learning experiences where there are exchanges, critiques, and sharing of information and points of view.

Extend the Innovation 1.2

G. Brooke Lester

MOOCs

Typically, MOOC refers to a "massive open online course" of the type offered by Coursera and Udacity (both for-profit organizations). These are "open" in the sense that nondegree, nonresidential students can take the courses, but "closed" in the sense that they operate in a closed learning management system. Pedagogically, the learning model is not innovative: students view lectures, read texts, and accomplish forced-choice performances (e.g., multiple-choice, short-answer, essay). Some peer support and collaboration may be involved, either facilitated by the institution or generated by the learners. EdX offers a similar model, but it is nonprofit and uses open-source instructional technology. 2012 is often called "the year of the MOOC." Here, at the end of 2014, these MOOCs show signs of entering a period of self-assessment.

cMOOCs

These are the MOOCs that existed before "the MOOC." In fact, the term "MOOC" was coined in 2008, to describe something *fundamentally different* to the then-yet-unimagined Coursera/Udacity model. In these open courses, learners create their own open online spaces for accomplishing real-world per-

formances relevant to their own contexts, and for mutual interaction (facilitated by the use of social media). A course hub on the open Web provides subject-matter-related course content and aggregate learner performances. In the years following the 2012 MOOC "boom," some "cMOOC-ers" have begun to abandon the term "MOOC" in favor of "distributed learning," "connected learning," and similar alternatives. An excellent recent example of a cMOOC is "Connected Courses."[2]

---

2. QR code URL: "Connected Courses," 9/15/2014–12/14/2014: http://connectedcourses.net.

xMOOCs

A term for the Coursera/Udacity model, coined by the "cMOOC" crowd to distinguish the original, connectivist MOOCs from this later, very different, model.

Collaborating with a teacher outside your institution works best, in my view, because it enables the "sharpening" of the proverbial "saw" in a lower-stakes relationships than working with colleagues from your own department or institution. Both members of a teaching team can reflect on their teaching practices to build up their strengths and expertise. If this happens across related disciplines, so much the better. With networked collaborations, it is not only that learners benefit in turn from a teacher's development; their teachers thereby also give them a similar context and dynamics to improve their learning. And so, in collaborative networked pedagogical development, participating teachers are able to marshal the collective strengths of their personal experience, teaching style, knowledge background, research interests, and usage of technology for teaching and learning.

Extend the Innovation 1.3

Christopher J. Duncanson-Hales

One of the real challenges for those of us beginning academic teaching careers is the almost total lack of formal pedagogical formation. A 2011 survey of university faculty by the Higher Education Research Institute at UCLA revealed that only 45.6 percent of those surveyed indicated that "to a great extent" they felt that the training they received in graduate school prepared them well for their role as a faculty members. When asked if they felt their graduate training prepared them to mentor new faculty, only 16.8 percent responded positively.[3] These responses reveal the real challenges that new faculty experience as they try to develop effective teaching and learning practices through further training and mentorship. Collaborating with a teacher outside of your institution not only enables provides professional development, but for new faculty, it has the potential to deepen the pool of potential mentors to help us continue to grow into our vocation as educators. The "lower-stakes relationship," that collaborating with a teacher outside your institution, creates a safe place beyond departmental egos and politics, where young faculty can continue to develop effective teaching and learning practices. As Loewen notes, the future of education—and I would add, to a lesser extent, the past—is social. One of the real advantages of using collaborative networked teaching and learning is that it builds these safe, mentoring relations between experienced and less experienced faculty.

---

3. Sylvia Hurtado, et al., *Undergraduate Teaching Faculty: The 2010–1011 Heri Faculty Survey* (Los Angeles: Higher Education Research Institute, 2012), 15, http://www.heri.ucla.edu/facPublications.php.

With the heightened importance of effective communication, the movement away from isolation toward collaboration provides a means of contextualizing learning that otherwise presents itself to students as collapsed. Michael Wesch introduced the idea of "context collapse"[4] to describe what the Internet does to information. It is not so much that context is destroyed, but that there is too much of it. Unable to support the weight of too much context, information collapses into one-dimensionality. This is why I am not asking for the classroom to open wide onto the public domain. Instead, the sovereignty of the classroom needs to be compromised by negotiations that enrich the context of the information being exchanged by teachers and learners.

There are many interests at play in using technology for teaching and learning. I am not interested in exploring these, other than to make an important note about the philosophy that is indicated by collaborative networked teaching and learning. Campus administrations and departments in North America almost entirely use the same terminology with reference to technology that might be used for teaching and learning. They call it "information technology" (IT), and this institutional trend leads to "campus IT departments." A collaborative networked philosophy requires thinking of ICT as something other than a synonym for IT. The "C" in ICT usually stands for "communication"—thus, information and communication technology. The emphasis on communication is missing in most campus deployments of "IT," and the imaginary space within which those technologies operate is limited to the passage of information. As I noted above, simply opening the classroom to more information causes context collapse rather than classroom enrichment. If that technology is conceived of as a means to facilitate communication, and there is an overt emphasis on making that communication happen in real time, then there is the possibility for context-enriched learning. Such an approach to campus technology can thereby also put emphasis upon other "Cs" in ICT: collaboration, context, communication, cultural knowledge, and—even though the "C" is inside the word—intercultural skills.

A Pedagogy of Recognition

The inclusion of "intercultural" in the Cs is very important for the philosophy of collaborative networked teaching and learning. I suggest that this emphasis on real-time communication across geographical distances helps establish what I call a "pedagogy of recognition." The idea springs from the essay "A Politics of Recognition" by the philosopher Charles Taylor.[5] Taylor suggests that identities in contemporary society are formed via dialogue and interchange. There is no unitary self in this sense; rather, there are social processes that enable identities to emerge. If Taylor is correct, then collaborative networked education provides both teachers and learners with a profound means by which they might define themselves in relation to others. In the Canadian political context to which Taylor often speaks,

---

4. Michael Wesch, "Context Collapse," July 31, 2008, http://mediatedcultures.net/youtube/context-collapse/.
5. Charles Taylor. "A Politics of Recognition," http://www.cs.cmu.edu/~mdr2/classes/readings/taylor.rtf.

the politics of recognition plays a role in "interculturalism." I see collaborative networked teaching and learning as an important means to realize the moments of intercultural development.

Taylor makes an analogy between the development of identity and that of language. Just as no one owns his or her own language and language is not of an individual's making, so, too, identity. I would take this further and also argue that the same is to be stated of knowledge. Knowledge is constructed socially, too, and so I see a clear connection between the theory of developmental psychology from Jean Paiget and the more explicitly education-oriented theory of constructivism from Lev Vygotsky.[6] The important realization from a contextualized learning experience, and particularly of collaborative networked learning sessions, is that your knowledge and identity are not your own. This metacognitive realization is worth repeating, and it leads to some important intercultural insights that lend themselves toward the development of intercultural skills.

The first realization is that of cultural embeddedness. Both the planning and the experience of the collaborative networked learning session can easily lead learners to realize that their context is not privileged over that of others. By facilitating interactions as peers, teachers may help learners discover their "embeddedness" in a unique language and culture that requires representation to others through negotiation, translation, and communication through other forms of mediation. All of this brings the constructed and embedded nature of knowledge into relief. No teacher or learner "owns" knowledge any more than he or she does identity, language, or culture.

I think it is important that teachers press home the specific "double-hosting" nature of networked collaborations so that learners can realize the intercultural dimensions of their learning experience. They are not penetrating or colonizing some far-away other's identity, culture, or knowledge. By interacting with others through media technology in a learning experience of being both host and guest, I have repeatedly witnessed students finding themselves in reciprocal, decentralized, and hospitable relationships with other learners. Since they have been led here in the classroom situation, the collaborating teachers can direct them toward the creation of a shared production such as an assignment or presentation. That important step is what leads learners to participate in substantive dialogue as well as develop their skills in virtual teamwork. From a philosophical perspective not far from Taylor's, I think this final stage of interclass learner collaboration makes possible something more than mere negotiation of differences. Instead, an important intercultural experience takes place that is best described as "solidarity."

I take this term from its use within Richard Rorty's book *Contingency, Irony, Solidarity*,[7] which describes what I think are the moments of interculturalism within collaborative networked teaching and learning. The initial experience of learning with geographically and culturally distant others is what helps learners

---

6. See, for example, Charlotte Hua Liu and Robert Matthews, "Vygotsky's Philosophy: Constructivism and Its Criticisms Examined," *International Education Journal* 6, no. 3 (July 2005): 386–99.
7. Richard Rorty, *Contingency, Irony, Solidarity* (Cambridge: Cambridge University Press, 1988), http://pages.uoregon.edu/koopman/courses_readings/rorty/rorty_CIS_full.pdf.

realize the contingency of their language, knowledge, and perspective. The work of communicating with each other across differences enables the "ironist" position: both learners and teachers will never, ultimately, "get it right." Where teaching and learning is a practice, there is not perfection; and the rejection of absolutes enables both teachers and learners to work more productively across all sorts of geo-social barriers. Solidarity is known pragmatically in the doing or making of something together. Solidarity is something utterly different from finding a minimum consensus. Creating together is an act of raising the bar and a matter of raising each other's game. The motive for co-creating in learning is to make something that "works," and solidarity nicely describes both the experience and the outcome of teaching and learning together.

The Three Pillars of Effective Social Learning

One of my objectives in this introductory chapter is to convince you of how much better it is to interact with other teachers and learnings in person rather than asynchronously. The transparency and communication required to make these sorts of learning experiences take place reinforce the intercultural pedagogy of recognition that I briefly outlined above. I also think that this approach to using technology in the classroom is best suited to enhance, rather than diminish, the strengths of smaller institutions in higher education.

My earlier reference to context collapse helps explain why and how too much of any good thing can be a bad thing. I think this is the case with social media and the treatment of communications technology as information-only technology. I am concerned that institutions lose their strengths when the technological context for teachers and learners' use of them enables practices of self-selection and opting out. Learners and teachers alike can "click out" of asynchronous communications almost any time they wish. While this capability is touted as the "anytime, anywhere" approach that should somehow revolutionize and "disrupt"[8] education, it is conventional thinking about the social potential of technology; moreover, the typical array of tools on most LMS services makes possible these most convenient disengagements. There is a serious problem with so-called social learning that provides students with so many easy ways to opt out.

How, then, might colleges best take advantage of the diffusion of technology and new media for effective social learning? I don't think that a turn to "massive" solutions is helpful. I think that effective social learning requires the movement toward a post-MOOC context for teaching and learning. I think this is the best answer for small institutions that cannot match the significant investments of capital, human resources, and time that have facilitated the proliferation of MOOCs.[9] Replicating or free-riding these initiatives literally and figuratively *encrypts* the strengths of any institution that subscribes to the "massive" as well as publicly "open" models

---

8. For an excellent mediation on "disruption," see Amod Lele's blog post, http://loveofallwisdom.com/blog/2014/02/of-disruptive-innovation/.
9. https://www.edsurge.com/n/2013-12-22-moocs-in-2013-breaking-down-the-numbers.

of IT-assisted education. And this is not to mention their encryption of finances, IT resources, and teaching excellence. Learners and teachers alike are better served by collaborations across networks with partners from around the world in order to provide local educational experiences.

My argument partly rests upon the idea that there are three pillars for effective social learning. One pillar resides in the emphasis on *in-person interactions*. Sociability is established strongly when communication is immediate. Good-faith expectations and respect for another is reinforced when people are able to respond to each other. Contextual learning is the outcome when teachers and learners communicate with real people who possess the ability for lively dialogue. While there are all sorts of reasons to value enrollment and retention, I think the best reason is pedagogical.

A second, related pillar is that of *real time*. Actual in-person communication only happens in real time. Asynchronous communications, from pen-pal exchanges to blog posts or wikis, are simply not as dynamic. Furthermore, real-time interactions underline the use of ICTs; all the complexities and opportunities that are afforded by "communication" and that happens most dynamically where recognition is an actual social process.

The third pillar of effective social learning is *collaboration*. In the remainder of this chapter, I will explain what I think to be the many and profound benefits of collaborative networked teaching and learning. At this point, it suffices to assert that social learning must be collaborative for it to have any sort of lasting impact for learning experiences. Collaboration in educational settings fosters essential skills that learners will need in the workplace. And collaboration, particularly of the co-hosting kind, makes possible the recognition of others that makes learning intercultural.

A History of Collaborative Networked Teaching and Learning

There are many educators who have arrived at the same conclusion as me. Each of us has come to this realization honestly. My experience began as a sessional lecturer at McGill University, and then as a faculty member in the department of humanities at Vanier College, also in Montreal. My first teaching assignment at McGill was to co-teach a course. The first time around, my colleague and I arranged the course in the way that so many students craft poor presentations: we each took separate responsibility for a section and met at the end of the semester. Over the next two semesters, we worked out a team-teaching rhythm where we were both present for each class session. The course began to "work" when we stopped simply alternating and actually began communicating with each other in the classroom. We brought something new to the learning experience through lively exchange of perspectives, debates, counterarguments, and differing disciplinary specializations. My first professional experiences therefore turned me on to collaborative teaching.

Vanier College is a small, English-language institution in Montreal with an emphasis on general education across all of its programs. I conceive of learning at Vanier as "liberal arts lite," since no graduate leaves without experiencing several classes in literature and the humanities with fewer than forty students. My experience with collaborative networked teaching and learning began in earnest at Vanier, where intercollegial team teaching was at an experimental phase. There were team-taught classes hosted between Vanier College and CÉGEP de Sept-Îles, about five hundred miles to the east of Montreal on the north shore of the Gulf of St. Lawrence. A rather small class of thirty learners at Vanier was paired with Sept-Île's class of ten. I was "hooked" after team-teaching an entire semester with my colleague, André Alizzi. I found a close colleague in André, with whom I have continued to work despite never actually meeting him corporeally!

Over the last six years the "virtual team-teaching" project expanded to involve over thirty teachers and their students at five colleges. As such, it has become a "virtual team-teaching network" that facilitates the collaborations of teachers to provide unique, real-time learning experiences. Aside from a yearly debriefing and training workshop, the participating teachers in the network never meet physically. The collaborative work that the teachers do together online serves as the starting point for thinking about how to design interactive learning experiences.

 In 2007, two teachers at different Quebec colleges (Vanier College and CÉGEP de Sept-Îles) experimented with real-time collaborative networked teaching. Successive teachers at both institutions participated in the experiment, which began to encompass multiple colleges in Canada and abroad. The Virtual Team Teaching Network is the result of that ongoing effort to support collaborative networked teaching and learning.[10]

My participation in and eventual leadership of the Virtual Team Teaching Network is not unique. By word of mouth and meeting other educators at conferences, I have found other self-started and institutional initiatives. In each case, there is a slow process where the idea of a collaborative networked teaching and learning initiative takes place and then becomes normalized. The process often starts out with an initial phase of ad hoc collaborations. These are very fragile and rarely make their way to becoming something regularized. My hope is that readers of this book will be able to achieve this first phase with fewer individual heroics and more collaborative coordination within participating institutions. Each partnership or network can eventually move toward a managed process, and the later chapters in this book are meant to outline suggestions for a clear and workable standard process. I am not expecting these managed processes to be followed exactly but, rather, defined and refined according to the perspectives and needs of the specific context for collaborative networked teaching and learning. Ideally, although I have

---

10. QR code URL: https://sites.google.com/site/vttnreve/.

not yet experienced this myself, collaborations of this sort can become institutionally normalized. At such a point in time, the standard processes are tested and improved upon in a deliberate manner so that the entire structure of the collaborative network is optimized. As I noted, this final phase of maturity is not something I have seen with my own eyes.

Why Should I Do This?

Becoming involved in a collaborative endeavor needs to have clearly definable benefits for everyone involved. The benefits of collaborative networked teaching and learning are not directly fiscal, but they are definitely organizational. I think there are very good reasons to embark on a collaborative project like this if you or your institution cares about teaching excellence or the cultivation of a positive and creative working environment.

Benefits for Teachers

Collaborative networked teaching cultivates attitudes that are essential for a thriving teaching practice:

- Collegiality
- Optimism
- Cooperation
- Tolerance
- Openness to diversity
- Adaptability
- Interest in problem solving

Collaborative networked teaching directly fosters teaching excellence, which is always an integrative enterprise that cross-links the various capabilities held by effective educators:

- Creates an understanding of instructional design.
- Demonstrates connections between and among institutional silos.
- Establishes or connects to an inter-institutional community of practice.
- Helps align the goings-on of the classroom to the institutional mission or goals.
- Cultivates knowledge of one's own institutional procedures, internal subcultures, and workflows.
- Exposes teaching and learning to different educational systems and institutional cultures.

- Assists in the revival or actualization of internationalization within the curriculum.

Benefits for Learners

As with so many things that go on "behind the curtain" in higher education, the learners in your classroom do not have the potential to benefit from your background work until it is put into action. Planning and delivering a collaborative networked learning experience is something unique:

- Provides experiential and contextual learning within the classroom.
- Models collaborative learning, where seeing the teacher's example leads to effective social learning.
- Demonstrates to learners how teacher-to-teacher interactions translate directly to their in-class experience.
- Establishes practical language-use skills.
- Develops media and technology literacy in a hands-on manner.
- Delivers course content through other learners' perspectives.
- Cultivates intercultural sensibilities and competencies through the encounter of regional and/or cultural differences.
- Instructs learners how to initiate effective working partnerships.
- Builds relationships and networks to sustain current learning and to create future opportunities.
- Cultivates interest and motivation for internships or international experience.
- Validates differences within the classroom and institution (cultural, national, religious, ideological, etc.).

Is This Really for Me? Where Does It Work Best?

I am quite sure that if you have picked up this book, then you are a good candidate. However, there are three points to consider when contemplating whether a collaborative networked project is "right" for you. First, any teacher open to others' opinions is right for this job. Second, a teacher who enjoys experimenting with different teaching approaches in the classroom will not only be open to opinions but also interested in acting upon them. Third, if you fit the first two then you are likely suited to the third: an educator has "the right stuff" if she or he is willing to introduce different media and technologies into the classroom. An extreme technophile who does not meet the first two points, however, is definitely not a good candidate.

Profile of the Collaborative Networked Teacher

Are you able to answer the following questions positively?

- Do you think that your teaching and knowledge would benefit from working with a colleague in another institution or from another geographical region?
- Do you teach a course that would be enhanced by widening its cohort beyond your institution?
- Do you teach a course that would be enhanced by interaction with learners in other geographic regions?
- Are you willing to practice cross-cultural sensitivity? You will need to interact with various:
    - cultures
    - geographic locations
    - institutions
    - disciplines
- Are you reasonably aware of how to negotiate power differentials with others?
- Are you reasonably aware of how to negotiate power differentials among learners?
- Do you have the ability to multitask in the classroom?
- Are you tolerant of uncertainty in outcomes in your teaching?
- Are you willing to diverge from the "usual" (your syllabus, traditions, colleagues, institution, textbook offerings)?
- Can you dedicate your time to a reflective procedure into your teaching? That is, are you willing to record and document your teaching throughout the semester?

Profile of the Collaborative Networked Teaching and Learning Institution

The chapter on "the details" outlines the important considerations that are "behind the curtain" of your own teaching practice. A successful collaborative effort must pay attention to the goings-on at your institution that are typically unseen by you and many others. Are you able to answer the following questions positively?

- Am I able to articulate how such a collaboration directly supports my department's goals?
- Am I able to articulate how such a collaboration directly supports my institution's strategic goals?
- Do I think that my institution will clearly support collaboration with a teacher at another institutions?
- Is there an international office or internship office with staff whose expertise could be utilized to support me, informally or formally?

- Is my department's curriculum committee open to minor alterations in my syllabus?
- Am I able to garner the support of stakeholders at my home institution (colleagues, chair, dean, IT services staff)?
- Would my institution ever provide me with time and resources to design, develop, and deliver collaborative learning experiences?

While it is important to answer all these questions in the affirmative, the last question in this list is not always a "deal-breaker." The last question is for you, rather than your institution, since you should not embark on a collaborative networked teaching project if you are unwilling to do so without release or other kinds of compensatory measures.

Challenges for Collaboration, Networking, Teaching, and Learning and the Keys for Success

While not wishing to be a pessimist, I do not want to propose collaborative networked teaching and learning as a panacea. Like anything worthwhile in education, this approach to enriching the classroom presents challenges to the educator. The introduction of new technologies or applications into the classroom should be done with the utmost skepticism and reticence, rather than enthusiasm and adoration. Any difficulty faced in collaborative work is rarely solved by asynchronous communications such as emails, texts, or chats. The most effective path to resolving any difficulty is that of real-time social interaction. And for this reason, I cannot emphasize enough how important it is to use face-to-face communication over the Web. This is the most significant challenge, scheduling face-to-face communication. Here are the others:

- *Discussing demands and costs with your collaborator, colleagues, and superiors* (time, thought, finances, equipment). Frank conversations about your needs can be difficult, but essential. The immediate assumption may be that this is expensive; this concern can be addressed by following a best practice in networked collaborations: use existing technologies at your institutions. Another way of stating this is that all the stakeholders at your institution must be aware of what you are doing.
- *Ensuring that your collaboration partner is accomplishing these items, too.* This is not simple, because cultural differences in communication may lead to false assumptions about what is or is not happening at your partner's institution.
- *Addressing difficulties and/or negative experiences with technology inside and outside the classroom.* Since you are likely doing something experimental, it is important to realize that errors will happen. The chapter on "the details" contains important tips for avoiding these difficulties as well as what to do when they arise.

- *Facing administrative or bureaucratic barriers is a very real possibility.* The arrangement of teaching in real time with a partner in another institution (and time zone?!) is not easy. In fact, this might be the most difficult task to accomplish in the entire book! There can be problems in scheduling or provincial closed-mindedness to collaboration at other levels in your institution, and you will need to bring all your collaborative capabilities to bear in order to find the flexibility you need to make your class happen!
- *You may very well face challenges in your or your partner's infrastructures.* Not every institution provides or prioritizes bandwidth or equipment for classrooms. Thorough testing and experimentation will help address some of these scenarios. On the other hand, your voice may provide the rationale or support for an improvement initiative that was looking for a reason to happen!
- *Disruption or a lack of continuity greatly interferes with collaboration, and these dynamics take a different for from one institution to the next.* A change in department chair, dean, or provost may lead to a sudden loss of support. Sometimes there are last-minute changes in teaching loads, course schedules, and room assignments. And for those who do adjunct teaching, there may be a definite lack of year-to-year continuity. These external factors can seriously derail a collaborative project.
- *Other people's minds are nearly impossible to read, and this can create a problem if you make assumptions.* The best way to avoid failures of expectations is to not assume that others will know what you need, what you are doing, and when it should be done. Clear and transparent communication that is face to face and on a regular basis will win the day when it comes to successful collaborations within your institution, with the learners in your class and with your partners.

Chapter Response I— *G. Brooke Lester*
How Did We Get to Here?

I don't know about you, but I usually don't see the fork in the road at the time I take it. It's typically only looking back that I can say, "Huh. Made a choice there." Or, occasionally, "Huh. Made a *meaningful* choice there."

As 2008 slid into 2009, a recent addition to the rank of PhDs and already-longtime member of the adjunct-faculty class, I read a blog post—I suppose for me in that year it must have been a blog post, rather than a tweet, or a Facebook status update—by Dr. A. K. M. "Akma" Adam, recommending his readers' attention to a then-recent video by Michael Wesch. Wesch, associate professor of cultural anthropology at Kansas State University, had just uploaded to YouTube his presentation "A Portal to Media Literacy" (2008), following his "The Machine is Us/ing Us" (2007). Both presentations concern learning and the digitization of text, exploring how the hyperlink, especially with the help of RSS (allowing us to "feed" Web content from one place to another), allows information—once hard to find, tucked into nesting drawers of categories into single locations—to live in virtually infinite numbers of places at once. The task for learners is no longer to *find* information but, rather, to cope with a world in which information has become ubiquitous. For example, learners can aggregate "feeds" of Web content that bears desired keywords or tags. "The Machine is Us/ing Us" also celebrates that learners are able, not only to navigate and aggregate Web content, but to create it, contributing to and becoming part of the "machine" and its ubiquity.

Experimenting with Wesch's ideas and methods, I began to incorporate into my face-to-face courses substantive elements of online collaborative learner interaction, in particular by asking my learners to create their own blogs and wikis outside of our institutional learning management systems ("LMSes," such as Blackboard or Moodle). Using RSS aggregation tools like Yahoo Pipes and aggregation sites like NetVibes, I would "feed" their blog posts and wiki contributions into a shared hub, usually a set of pages in our LMS. Later, their "distributed" activity would come to include the creation and annotation of socially shared Web bookmarks (using sites like Diigo), and, of course, eventually tweets and Twitter chats, all of this also aggregated into a shared course "hub" through the miracle of RSS.

My experiments led naturally into opportunities for online teaching and learning, and eventually facilitating faculty professional development in the pedagogies taking shape around digitally mediated learning. When I am not researching and teaching my academic subject matter (Hebrew Bible/Old Testament), I am engaged in the research and practices oriented toward questions like, "Why do we teach online courses? Why do learners enroll in them?" "How do I translate what I already know about good teaching into an online environment?" "What makes me confident that what I know about 'good teaching' is true?" "What is economically just (or unjust) about the ways we're teaching? About the ways we are considering teaching?" "What is learning, how do we know learning has happened, and how do we assess performances that demonstrate learning?" "How soon before I have to read another higher-education-related 'Something-Something-Disruption' or 'Is X the Death of Y?' opinion piece?" "Why do people keep reading Thomas Friedman and David Brooks on higher education?"

To engage these questions, I collaborate with faculty colleagues concerning their practices. I take certification programs in online teaching. I also observe and participate in more informal online learning events, many of which are built on a model that evokes my earliest brushes with digital learning. These include events like MOOC MOOC, ETMOOC, Rhizomatic Learning, and, most recently, Connected Courses. In these courses, learners are helped to build their own platforms in which to create in response to course prompts. (At its most simple, this can just be a Wordpress or Blogger blog, and maybe a Twitter account.) Learners make things, share them, interact concerning the things they make, forming communities of inquiry and of mutual support. My pedagogical mind map begins to be populated not only by areas marked with terms like "constructivism" and "play," but by ill-defined regions like "maker culture," "less yack, more hack," "distributed learning," and—increasingly—variants on "MOOC": MOOCs, cMOOCs, xMOOCs, corporate MOOCs. My inquiries eventually led me back to the neighborhood of that fork in the road, the one I hadn't quite noticed while I was taking it.

Back in that same year of 2008 (remember, *this was 2008!*), unknown to me at the time, the MOOC was born.[11] That is to say: Dave Cormier, in an effort to describe a particular learning event created and facilitated by George Siemens and Stephen Downes, coined the term "MOOC," or "massive open online course." The learning event was "Connectivism and Connected Knowledge," or "CCK08."[12] Students for this course included a small "core" group of University of Manitoba degree students, plus over two thousand learners participating in the course free of charge. As with many of these courses (MOOC MOOC, Rhizomatic Learning, Connected Courses), the course design was a conscious reflection of the subject matter. "Connectivism" describes an approach to learning which holds, as Stephen Downes says, ". . . that knowledge is distributed across a network of connections, and therefore that learning consists of the ability to construct and traverse those networks."[13]

For these pioneers in distributed learning, what makes a course a "MOOC" is *how* it understands learning (some form of connectivism) and, relatedly, *the way that it scales.* While begun with a Web "hub," the action of the course is the learners'

---

11. Stephen Downes, "A True History of the MOOC" (audio recording), http://www.downes.ca/presentation/300.
12. Stephen Downes, "The MOOC Guide: CCK08—The Distributed Course," https://sites.google.com/site/themoocguide/3-cck08---the-distributed-course.
13. Stephen Downes, "What Connectivism Is," http://halfanhour.blogspot.co.uk/2007/02/what-connectivism-is.html.

building of a traversable network. The intentional weakness of the center[14] means that the action of the course is less about interactions between the learners and the hub, and more about the knowledge built among the nodes on the network. Or, using Dave Cormier's rhizomatic metaphor (originating in Gilles Deleuze and Felix Guattari's *The Thousand Plateaus*[15]), the course is about the unpredictable "lines of flight" that shoot out from the established network of roots.

To anticipate the next chapter somewhat, Loewen will observe that "the classroom should be the place where the creation of knowledge is experienced rather than where teachers present finished products to be quickly consumed." For the connectivist educator, the network should be the place where learners' performances create knowledge rather than demonstrate information consumed.

---

14. "ETMOOC: About," http://etmooc.org/sample-page/.
15. Gilles Deleuze and Felix Guattari, *The Thousand Plateaus: Capitalism and Schizophrenia* (Minneapolis: University of Minnesota Press, 1987).

Chapter Response II—*Christopher J. Dunanson-Hales*

Finding Your "Plan B": Asynchronous and Synchronous Technology

In 1994, Dale Hubert began the Flat Stanley Project in Ontario, Canada. This literacy project was an asynchronous, pen-pal-type project where children would create their own Flat Stanley paper cutouts and mail them to friends and family around the globe.

At the time, my mother-in-law was teaching kindergarten in Mindemoya, Ontario. Mindemoya is a small village on Manitoulin Island that is approximately a four-hour drive from the closest major population centers. By mailing and receiving Flat Stanley and, more importantly, maintaining a journal of Flat Stanley's adventures, Doreen's students in this relatively isolated, rural Ontario community were able to connect asynchronously with children and communities all over the world.

Fast forward to 2014, fifty years after Flat Stanley made his first journey by snail mail: hitchBOT, a 3G- and Wi-Fi-enabled robot cobbled together from a bucket, some swimming pool toys, rubber boots, and electronics, embarked on a synchronous version of Flat Stanley's adventures. Developed by Dr. David Harris Smith (McMaster University) and Dr. Frauke Zeller (Ryerson University), hitchBOT was conceived as a collaborative art project to investigate whether robots can trust human beings. Through its charm and trustworthiness, aided by artificial intelligence and a user-friendly interface design, including speech recognition and processing, hitchBOT successfully hitchhiked from Halifax, Nova Scotia, to Victoria, British Columbia, with stops and detours along the way.[16]

Flat Stanley. Photo: Miles Goodhew (CC-by-SA license, Flickr).

For our purposes, what it more interesting than the successful completion of these projects is how they demonstrate the differences and challenges of asynchronous and synchronous technology. With the example of Flat Stanley, students were

---

16. "Meet Hitchbot—a Hitchhiking Robot Traveling from Coast to Coast This Summer," *News & Events*, July 16, 2014, http://www.ryerson.ca/news/media/spotlight/hitchbot/20140716-media-release-hitchbot.html#center_generichtml.

physically connected with a globally traveled paper cut-out that was physically passed through a chain of children's hands, connecting classrooms to classrooms. While the delayed gratification of physically holding Flat Stanley is not without value, this value is limited by the time and distance Flat Stanley would need to travel, the willingness of Flat Stanley recipients to forward him to his next destination, the reliability of postal service in certain regions of the world, and the robustness of the paper/cardboard medium of which Flat Stanley was composed.

Unlike Flat Stanley, the journey of hitchBOT was only ever physically experienced by those individuals who, happening upon this robot at the side of the road, gave him a ride. While for these individuals there was a similar physical connection as experienced by passing Flat Stanley along, in general, these physical connections were limited to those who happened upon and recognized hitchBOT's need for a ride. It is the use of modern technology that distinguishes hitchBOT's cross-country trek from Flat Stanley's global sojourn. Unlike Flat Stanley, with hitchBOT there was no delay in gratification for those following this robot's journey across Canada.

HitchBOT's onboard technology, including its computer processing unity, artificial intelligence algorithms, and communication technology allowed it to live tweet, Facebook, and blog on its adventures to more than eighty thousand Facebook and Twitter followers.[17]

In addition to this social-media presence, hitchBOT's story was picked up—asynchronously I might add—and featured on a variety of local, national, and global news media providers, thus extending its virtual journey far beyond the physical kilometers of his cross-Canada hitchhiking.

With that said, hitchBot's journey provides a cautionary tale for collaborative networked teaching and learning. At one point during hitchBOT's journey, the tweets and Facebook posts stopped. Some openly wondered if hitchBOT's journey, somewhere in the wilds of northern Ontario, had come to a tragic and premature end. As it turned out, hitchBOT was fine, having only experienced a temporary communication blackout due to the lack of Internet and 3G cell phone infrastructure and connectivity. HitchBOT's silence reminds us that, while promising, there are limitations to relying on modern technology for synchronous learning. HitchBOT's communication blackout reminds us, as noted in this chapter, of the importance asynchronous preparation and workable Plan Bs have for collaborative networked teaching and learning.

---

17. QR code URL: http://www.hitchbot.me/storify/.

Chapter 2

The Collaboration

Nathan Loewen

> **At a Glance**
>
> Doing collaborative teaching involves finding a working partner. This chapter discusses the process of finding a partner.
>
> - Collaborative networked pedagogy as "co-hosting"
> - Finding a collaborator
> - Building the collaboration
> - Paying attention to intercultural sensitivity
> - Communicating effectively and efficiently

Collaborative Networked Pedagogy and "Co-Hosting"

My first job after graduating with a bachelor's degree in religious studies was as an apprentice electrician. Within months, I was filling sixty- to seventy-hour workweeks with learning about building codes, wiring techniques, schematics, and the complex dynamics of a fast-paced worksite. Over the next five years, I quickly realized why apprenticeships are central to a tradesperson's education: seeing something in action is an effective means of learning, particularly when the learner is

---

*QR code URL: http://www.hybridpedagogy.com/journal/phenomenology-participation-derrida-future-pedagogy/

expected to follow the demonstration correctly from then on. To do otherwise threatened my job or my safety.

In comparison to the worksite, college classrooms are typically generic and lack context. Labs for the sciences are the exception to the expectation that campus classrooms support a daily succession of courses like philosophy, biology, economics, and religious studies. The challenge, from my experience, is to make the classroom work as effectively for learning as the tradesperson's jobsite. Some kind of practical communicative experience is required for effective learning in any discipline that requires a learner to recognize the basic elements of a field of knowledge, organize the main components into coherent patterns, and produce a synthesis of the main components. And while I myself constantly use active learning to develop these competencies in my courses, I do think that the experience of collaborative networked learning sessions enriches the effectiveness of reaching my overall course objectives.

The contextual and experiential learning involved in a collaborative networked learning session takes place by digitally transforming the classroom. Between the generic classrooms is a third space that emerges through the co-hosting planned by the collaborating teachers. The emergence of this space can be represented by a Venn diagram.

The third space is the overlap between the two classrooms that is achieved by using various technologies and Web-based tools. It emerges when teachers collaboratively design sessions whereby they and their learners construct and act within the co-hosted space. The success of the session depends greatly upon the teachers' ability to model effectively what the learners are to demonstrate. The nature of the collaborative networked session lends itself well to the exercise of practical communication about a given field of knowledge, particularly when learners are expected to work together in synthesizing components of that discipline. This kind of social-learning pedagogy is focused on co-hosting learning.

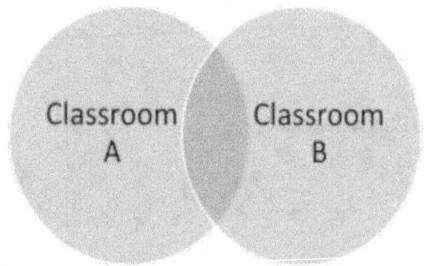

Adapted from "Opening Up the Classroom" by Sharon Coyle and Nathan Loewen.[1]

Effective Collaboration and Jacques Derrida's "Hospitality"

The discussions of "hospitality" in the works of Jacques Derrida (1930–2004) are instrumental to understanding successful collaborative networked teaching and

---

1. Sharon Coyle and Nathan Loewen, "Opening Up the Classroom: Why and How You Might Try a Bit of Virtual Team Teaching!" in T. Bastiaens and G. Marks, eds., *Proceedings of World Conference on E-Learning in Corporate, Government, Healthcare, and Higher Education 2012* (Chesapeake, VA: AACE, 2012), 97–101.

learning. Derrida's concern was to address the difficulties in French society regarding its colonial legacy of the past and the social diversity of the present. As an Algerian of Jewish descent, Derrida experienced firsthand how France conferred legal citizenship to peoples from its former colonies while French society did not accord those people recognition or social access. Derrida was concerned to reframe thinking around cultural and religious difference that often balked at and fetishized "the Other" as somehow strange, unfamiliar, or improper. He found an answer in the concept of "hospitality."

Derrida's many works addressing the topic of hospitality[2] explore how differences may be preserved in the meeting of two groups. A good host invites, and does not force, guests to interact. Neither hosts nor guests expect each other to be the same. A guest is neither an intruder nor intrusive. All of the guest–host and host–guest interactions are characterized by mutual respect, generosity, and reciprocity. Even more so, however, is the trust upon which these relationships are based. Derrida writes: ". . . hospitality must wait, extend itself toward the other, extend to the other the gifts, the site, the shelter and the cover; it must be ready to welcome. . . . the opposite is also nevertheless true. Simultaneously and irrepressibly true: to be hospitable is to let oneself be overtaken, *to be ready or not to be ready* . . . precisely where one is not ready to receive."[3]

Extend the Innovation 2.1

G. Brooke Lester

As my own institution makes its first overtures to potential partners, and we contemplate the "tangibles" of what Loewen describes as "mutual respect, generosity, and reciprocity," I keep returning to the novel (to me) and promising concept of the "gift economy."

Risking oversimplification, one can say that a "gift economy" is an arrangement in which the *giver* of a good or service, rather than the recipient, is considered to have the "better end of the deal." Giving the gift demonstrates the giver's prosperity and largesse; receiving the gift incurs the burden of indebtedness. In most understandings of the "gift economy," balance is not restored through a one-to-one or immediate recompense. Instead, balance is restored

---

2. See Jacques Derrida, *Margins of Philosophy*, trans. Alan Bass (Chicago: University of Chicago Press, 1982); idem, *The Politics of Friendship*, trans. George Collins (Brooklyn: Verso, 1996); idem, *The Other Heading: Reflections on Today's Europe* (Bloomington: Indiana University Press, 1992); idem, *Spectres of Marx: The State of the Debt, the Work of Mourning, and the New International*, trans. Peggy Kamuf (New York: Routledge, 1994); *Monolingualism of the Other; or, The Prosthesis of Origin*, trans. Patrick Mensah (Stanford: Stanford University Press, 1998); *Of Hospitality: Anne Dofourmantelle Invites Jacques Derrida to Respond*, Mieke Ball and Hent de Vries, eds. (Stanford: Stanford University Press, 2000); Derrida, *On Cosmopolitanism and Forgiveness* (New York: Routledge, 2001); idem, "Hospitality," in *Acts of Religion*, ed. and trans. Gil Anidjar (New York: Routledge, 2002), 356–420; idem, *Eyes of the University: Right to Philosophy 2*, trans. Jan Plug (Stanford: Stanford University Press, 2004); idem, *Sovereignties in Question: The Poetics of Paul Celan*, ed. Thomas Dutoit (New York: Fordham University Press, 2005).
3. Derrida, "Hospitality," 361.

through an eventual return gifting, not necessarily equivalent in terms of "market value" but of commensurable value in the more subjective terms of largesse. In this sort of reciprocity, one gives to another (or to the community) in the confidence that one will receive from that other (or from the community) at some point in the future. As an aggressive act, a participant in a gift economy might leverage her greater prosperity to make a large gift (a "potlatch"), placing on the recipient a burden beyond his ability to reciprocate; in this performative act, the giver subjugates the recipient. Partners aspiring to "mutual respect and generosity" (again quoting Loewen) will be careful to avoid "potlatching."

The concept of "gift economy" finds imaginative exploration by novelist Kim Stanley Robinson in his *Red Mars* science-fiction trilogy.[4] What equally imaginative exploration might it find in Loewen's guest–host and host–guesting networked classrooms?

Successful collaborative networked teaching and learning involves techniques that practice hospitality. Doing so requires an approach to teaching colleagues and learners that has co-hosting at its core. This does not involve the erasure or elision of foreignness or familiarity. Collaboration over networks across geographical distances is complex, and Derrida's conception of hospitality makes eminent sense of the complexity of how two groups may relate in the virtually co-hosted space.

"Hospitality" characterizes the attitude required for teaching via collaborative online teaching because the efforts involved in planning a collaborative session require teachers to be "open" not only to each other, but to whatever surprises arise from that collaboration. The processes of creating a session plan for learning involves real-time communication, which not only demands vulnerability, reciprocity, and mutuality of interactions, but also requires an openness to surprises, or what often are misrecognized as "failures" or "mistakes." The mutual respect offered each other in these instances is part of the recognition that all the participants are simultaneously foreigners and at home vis-à-vis each other's virtual presence. This is the kind of trust enacted by teachers and learners in the networked collaborative class sessions.

Co-hosting and Bakhtin's Dialogical Approach

The literary theory of Russian philosopher Mikhail Bakhtin (1895–1975) includes a theory of language that is useful for thinking about co-hosting because Bakhtin insists upon the unfinished nature of meaning. Adopting Bakhtin's concept of "dialogic expression" is a helpful addition to Derrida for co-hosting to "work." Bakhtin was wary of efforts, particularly by the modern state, to eradicate dialogue in favor of monologic expression. He saw this particularly at work in the efforts of the Soviet state's education regime. And while the Soviet Union no longer exists, there

---

4. Kim Stanley Robinson, *Red Mars* (New York: Spectra, 1993); idem, *Green Mars* (New York: Spectra, 1995); and idem, *Blue Mars* (New York: Spectra, 1997).

is sometimes a push within educational systems for monologism. Indeed, some of the thinking about diversity (social, cultural, ethnic, linguistic) includes a desire for monologue to be the resolution of diversity.[5]

Whenever the objective is "unity" or "let's get over our differences," any effort to guide or create a unified statis is monological. At first glance, these objectives seem benign and perhaps laudable, but they ultimately make the same mistake that Bakhtin saw in the Soviet ideology: dialogue and freedom is limited or constricted toward one perspective, conclusion, or viewpoint. Bakhtin argued for the importance of preserving dialogical expression because actual dialogue is never final or complete. This is precisely what makes exchanges of meaning capable of producing further responses. A successful dialogue can end in plurality.

Effective co-hosting requires a "dialogical approach," where "At any moment in the development of the dialogue there are immense, boundless masses of forgotten contextual meanings, but at certain moments of the dialogue's subsequent development along the way they are recalled and invigorated in renewed form (in a new context)."[6] In order for each class to host the other well in a networked context, the teachers must be conscious of the temptation to shut down freedom of communication by structuring the experience toward a consensus or necessary outcome. The objective in collaborative teaching is to grant learners the capacity to struggle with differences among themselves without the expectation that, in the end, someone will "lose" his or her contribution. In other words, Bakhtin's concept of dialogical expression helps us avoid zero-sum pedagogies in favor of win-win collaborations.

The Practice of Co-Hosting Is Not Perfect

I remain struck by an observation about medicine, granted to me by a gynecologist: "Doing good medicine is about practice and not perfection. Avoid any doctor who tells you otherwise!" I think the same can be said of hospitality in teaching. Derrida's explanation of hospitality, namely the readiness to not be ready, illustrates the openness by which an educator should approach networked collaborations. At every step along the way of collaborative work is an inescapable demand to create educational experiences where all the participants are simultaneously co-hosts and co-guests, and learners are able to realize this best when they experience synchronous connections with other groups.

When collaborating parties keep this in mind, they are better able to avoid adopting a lack of caution or personal comfort in order to achieve an outcome. Doing so inevitably leads to difficult scenarios for which neither party will have established an ability to absorb errors or adjust to the unexpected. Networked collaborations typically involve negotiating differences and meanings in a variety

---

5. I owe this contribution to discussions with Eric Lozowy, dean of the Faculty of Sciences and General Studies at Vanier College.
6. Mikhail Bakhtin, "Toward a Methodology for the Human Sciences," trans. Vern W. McGee, in *Speech Genres and Other Late Essays*, ed. Caryl Emerson and Michael Holquist (Austin: University of Texas Press, 1986), 170.

of contexts, and this is not only between collaborators and their institutions, but also within each collaborating teacher's institution. Asking for perfection in any of these contexts rarely leads to the flexibility that all stakeholders need to espouse to facilitate a synchronous collaborative learning session.

Communicating the importance of practice rather than perfection makes hospitality possible within the classroom during a collaborative session. I recall another pithy piece of wisdom offered by a collaborative teaching team: "kitchen not dinner."[7] Their point resonates with the emphasis on practice; learners disengage and check out very quickly in a networked learning session when the co-hosting practice is replaced by the presentation of a perfected product. Not even television does this anymore!

As a result, teachers not only need to model the practice of co-hosting but also to expect it of the learners. The level of communication and collaboration between the teaching partners needs to be focused on devising goals and activities that will create a similar context between the two networked classrooms. In order to establish these sorts of learning situations does require a strong partnership between the teachers.

Finding a Collaborator

Finding a good working partner and establishing an effective partnership is fundamental to successful social learning through networked collaboration. The remainder of this chapter is focused on creating a collaborative teaching team.

Extend the Innovation 2.2

Christopher J. Duncanson-Hales

Located in northern Ontario, the University of Sudbury and Laurentian University are committed to advancing postsecondary education among First Nation people on whose land these institutions were built. The reality in Canada, as is the case through much of North America, is that although the population of First Nation university-age young people is rising, this demographic continues to be underrepresented on our campuses. Collaborative networked teaching and learning provides an opportunity to address this gap.

One of the challenges faced by First Nation students is the need to leave their communities for extended periods to pursue university education. Collaborative networked teaching and learning is one means that can enable First Nation students to participate in university studies without leaving their communities. Indeed, First Nation education authorities are in many respects ahead of universities in their efforts to development collaborative networks for teaching and learning. One endeavor worth noting is the Kenjgewin Teg Educational Institute (KTEI) on Manitoulin Island. According to the institute's

---

7. Thanks to Holland Hopson and Jamey Grimes at the University of Alabama.

Website profile, KTEI is committed to the provision of educational services that complement First Nation's education delivery in meeting the needs of all learners in school and post-school programs. KTEI is a non-profit incorporated organization that serves a membership of eight First Nation communities: Aundeck Omni Kaning, Constance Lake, M'Chigeeng, Sagamok, Sheguiandah, Sheshegwaning, Whitefish River First Nation, and Zhiibaahasing First Nations. The Institute began with five staff and today has a complement of over eighteen personnel, plus many contractual staff. KTEI's primary function is to provide educational initiatives to its member population of 6,800+ people.[8]

KTEI accomplishes this mandate both by bringing contractual faculty in from Sudbury for live, face-to-face intensive programs and through synchronous video conferencing.

Finding a Suitable Partner

There are probably myriad parallels between online dating and the task of finding a suitable partner for collaborative teaching. In many instances, the discovery of someone both interested and willing to participate in a collaborative teaching project is a matter of luck, happenstance, and serendipity. Cases in my experience run the gamut from cold-call emails to curated match-making. Here are some possible means of finding "that special someone"!

- *Find a collaborative teaching initiative.* While this approach to teaching and learning is not widespread among North American institutions, there are some networks and programs that can be contacted. There is the Virtual Team Teaching Network in Canada and the Collaborative Online International Learning program at the State University of New York. The continued existence of these initiatives often depends on ongoing institutional interest, support, and efforts for normalization.

- *Search through Websites of foreign institutions.* An international collaboration is sometimes more feasible than a domestic one. International partners may be more interested and willing to be flexible in order to make a collaborative project work. If you think a specific region or country would provide an important perspective for your teaching, then the task of where to look becomes slightly simpler.

- *Contact whoever is responsible for internationalization at your institution.* As noted in chapter 1, creating an international collaborative partnership more than likely fulfills some of your institution's mission or strategic objectives. College internationalization is trending across higher education in North America, and your institution has likely assigned an internationalization portfolio to one of its administrators or to an entire office. You may find that there is an already-existing list of institutions,

---

8. http://www.ktei.net/history.html.

regions, or countries, and you may find motivated persons to support you in establishing contacts.

- *Determine whether you, your department, or faculty have contacts with other institutions.* You and your colleagues likely obtained your graduate degrees at different institutions. Some of them might have also participated in post-docs or other research activities associated with other institutions. Having a conversation—either one on one or at a group meeting—that explains your interest and goals may very well produce suggested collaborators with a strong potential for personal and professional relationships. This is common ground upon which you may build a collaboration.

- *Inquire about developing or ongoing projects.* By courteously and diplomatically conversing with senior administrators, such as your dean, you might find out about a collaborative or networked project that is ongoing or in the works. These are not only potential points of entry for you to find a partner, they also might be an opportunity to provide your institution with a complimentary and useful approach to inform their project about collaborative networked teaching and learning.

- *Learn whether your institution has "feeders."* Every institution has a promotions portfolio by which it seeks to gather strong prospects for incoming students. This usually includes a list of "feeder institutions" (e.g., community colleges, other institutions' undergraduate programs). The administrator or office tasked with cultivating this portfolio would likely welcome a discussion with you about forming a collaborative partnership with one of those institutions. You might tap into a mutual interest to raise or reinforce that relationship by raising awareness and potentially helping prospective applicants make a more informed transition to the next stage in their learning trajectory.

- *Scout out prospective partners at external events.* Every discipline in higher education has at least one academic association related to it at local, national, or international levels. Choosing to attend or participate in the annual meetings of these organizations provides you with an excellent opportunity to discover potential collaborators. Your scouting strategy may be simply to listen and observe, with an eye toward making a formal contact via email, or you might actively strike up conversations with potential partners at breaks or during receptions. You might find strong institutional support to attend these meetings if you discuss your objectives with your coordinator, dean, or international office.

- *Scout out prospective partners through academic involvements.* There is an ever-proliferating online presence of academic publishing related to your discipline. There are likely already several online journals, blogs, research groups, webinars, and workshops. Whether you take an active role in participating or organizing or only observe, these are opportunities to find common interests and Web-based abilities around which a prospective collaboration might be established.

- *Participate in social networking.* Since social learning is a key component of collaborative networked teaching and learning, you might find someone from among this self-selected group of online social seekers. The number of platforms for social networking are profligate, even for academics. The usual suspects (Facebook, Twitter, LinkedIn, Academia.edu) are good places to look, but you might also find potential partners on other social sites, such as Pinterest, Tumblr, Reddit, Scoop.it, Mashable, Publishthis, ResearchGate, and so forth.

These are only suggested pathways toward finding a collaborator. There are likely many others. In fact, you may have already found a collaborator through some other means. One important point to keep in mind is that administrators always see inter-institutional relationships as "delicate." Administrators of particular portfolios, such as internationalization, communications, or promotions, will at the very least take a cautious interest in what you are trying to do beyond the walled garden of the alma mater. Therefore, it is important to move deliberately and take the opportunity to inform the various stakeholders identified within all the bullet points above. (Please take the time to consider the relevant sections of chapter 6, "The Details.")

Once You Have Found a Suitable Partner

Do you think that you have found a collaborator? Congratulations! For some this is incredibly easy and for others it is quite the accomplishment. Hopefully, along the way, you have broadened your professional and academic network, too.

What follows are explanations of important considerations to keep in mind throughout the duration of your collaboration. In fact, the items below are crucial for both partners' awareness so that the collaboration can successfully make its way into the classroom and inform the experiences of your learners. And so there is nothing pedantic in suggesting that he or she also reads this book.

You will need to pay close attention to note cross-cultural sensitivities and power differences in every moment of your collaboration. This will be the case regardless of whether your collaboration is technically "international." There will be many cultural differences between among you, your partner, and the learners in your classes. Not only is this to be expected, but the existence of deep and possibly irreconcilable differences form the foundations of deep, contextual learning. If everyone agreed or came to the exact same outcomes in your planned activities for a collaborative networked learning session, then there would be a complete lack of perspective. For example, there will be varying disciplinary strengths and knowledge, and there will very likely be differences either in your personal technological know-how or technical support from your institutions. This will be the case throughout every negotiation of the collaborative project. Your partnership depends upon how you and your collaborator reflect upon each of these instances. Furthermore, your learners will experience the greatest benefit if you can build those kinds of metacognitive reflections into your session plans.

By paying careful attention to cross-cultural differences, your collaboration may lead to learning experiences that develop learners' competencies beyond mere knowledge of others toward the respectful engagement of others. The central product of your collaboration is the in-class networked learning session, where your learners are a "captive audience" and are less able simply to disengage from the collaborating group. Well-designed scenarios will enable learners to become each others' co-hosts, and thereby move past gazing and fascination toward actual engagement. The two-way communication facilitated by Web tools helps them recognize each other. This is the reflexive competency of being aware of being encountered by another.

I have written elsewhere about my philosophy that teaching demands an active relationship with social diversity.[9] There I describe a difference between negative tolerance, characterized as "not reproducing overt stereotypes,"[10] and positive tolerance. Positive tolerance is the active practice of awareness and negotiation of differences and divides. Negative tolerance solves the problem of difference and potential conflict by walking away or, in most cases today, self-selectively clicking away. Positive tolerance seeks out ways and means to actively create the conditions that diminish stereotyping, racism, and bigotry. Positive tolerance asks teachers to develop—for themselves and their learners—intercultural competencies that enable them to:

1. Experience and understand cultural diversity.

2. Actively engage collaborative skills.

3. Believe that ideas and things can be improved.

The conversations between you and your collaborator are the place where intercultural differences will first be experienced, and your partnership will also be the point of contact to address those intercultural negotiations that will inevitably develop through and during your collaborative networked teaching sessions. As noted above, your partnership can only be strengthened if you choose to integrate into your planning regular conversations on the topic of how your collaboration may develop intercultural competencies in your institutions.

---

9. Nathan Loewen, "La Pédagogie interculturelle: favoriser l'internationalisation dans le cadre d'une pédagogie de la tolérance positive" ("A Proposal to Support College Internationalization within a Pedagogy of Positive Tolerance"), *Pédagogie Collégiale* 26, no. 3 (Spring 2013): 29–34. An English-language version may be found at http://www.aqpc.qc.ca/UserFiles/File/pedagogie_collegiale/Loewen-vol26-3(A).pdf.

10. Wolfgang Höpken, "Learning to Live Together: Fighting Stereotypes from Textbooks to the Internet," in Daniel Laqua and Aurore Salinas, eds., *New Ignorances, New Literacies: Learning to Live Together in a Globalizing World* (Paris: UNESCO, 2005), 138–44, at 142, http://unesdoc.unesco.org/images/0013/001395/139524E.pdf.

What follows is a list of intercultural competencies that may be cultivated in your collaboration and that may form learning goals for your session plans:

- To communicate meaningfully to persons in other contexts.
- To notice others' contextual uses of language, behavior, or gestures.
- To adopt or adapt others uses of language, behavior, or gestures.
- To understand variations in how communication can be variously interpreted.
- To exercise resilience and forbearance in the face of social discomfort, difficulty, or conflict.
- To variously display "good faith" to others and perceive varying kinds of "good faith" in others.
- To recognize when another finds a topic difficult or sensitive.
- To assess the values, beliefs, and attitudes at play in the discussion of difficult or sensitive topics.
- To reflect on the constructed nature of personal and social identity through contact with others.
- To create new forms of personal and social expression.
- To take an interest in change and uncertainty.[11]

I suggest not only keeping these competencies in mind but also to actively seek to integrate these into the learning goals and activities for your collaborative networked sessions (for what I mean by "goals and activities," you can thumb forward to chapter 4, "The Content"). Doing so will make it more likely that your collaboration can create the kinds of "aha!" moments of learning in your sessions, where learners find themselves collaboratively exercising their creativity amongst each other without hijacking the project. The products created from these kinds of interactions are the foundation for creating links between individuals, societies, and institutions.

Building Your Collaborative Partnership

Your Personal Strengths

Among the most immediate benefits to collaboration that I regularly experience is how experiencing another's strengths "ups my game." Put another way, working with a teaching professional from another institutional situation in the context of networked collaboration is a win-win scenario for each other's professional

---

11. Adapted from UNSECO, *Intercultural Competencies: Conceptual and Operational Framework*, ed. Intersectoral Platform for a Culture of Peace and Non-Violence and the Bureau of Strategic Planning (Fontenoy, France: UNESCO, 2013), http://unesdoc.unesco.org/images/0021/002197/219768e.pdf.

development. Where Steven Covey discusses "sharpening your saw" as the habit of an effective person, working well with one's partner can be an experience of co-sharpening. As with intercultural sensitivity, you and your learners will benefit when your collaboration makes this a regular topic of discussions. The question of how to enable effective social learning amongst your classes is helpfully addressed by your partnership's active attention to how you might build upon each other's strengths.

Having someone to share in developing your strengths and understanding your weaknesses is something that may best be done with someone outside your institution. You or your partner may already be familiar with various means by which these can be identified. The reliable standbys in my experience are the Myers-Briggs Type Indicator and the Enneagram Personality System. There are many others, no doubt. Both are useful for self-knowledge and reflection on what might be one's growing edges. They are quite "context agnostic," too, in the sense that these self-evaluation tools are not explicitly developed for the industries of self-help, business management, or employment services. Of course, the decision to use tools like these is up to you and your partner.

Your Working Styles

In any case, your partnership will greatly benefit from a discussion about work styles. There should be some discussion about your preferred work styles. Differences in work styles is an asset for a virtual team that reflects on itself, but there may be need for some negotiated compromise. The impetus for your partnership is likely due to shared disciplinary and/or pedagogical interests, and your work styles should be adjusted in light of the collaboration's goal of producing networked learning experiences.

There are several differences that can be used to the team's advantage. Above all, even though both partners are considering entry into a project that involves technology, you have different experiences and knowledge of computers, smartphones, projectors, videoconferencing units, large screens, cameras, and various online applications. Here is where your differences are greater than the sum of their constituent elements. What seems obvious or practical to one may be subject to the other's caution, or both of you may need to pool your knowledge to adapt a technology to the needs of your goals and activities. Perhaps one of you relies upon ideas or data, whereas the other is a "people person." Or there is a difference in how you approach risk or structure. Or, it may be that one of you is project and deadline oriented whereas the other prefers to work with open-ended processes. I do not mention teaching style in this section, partly because each member of a team will be radically adjusting her or his teaching style to suit the context of a synchronous collaborative learning session.

Your Institution's Style

In addition to the intercultural discussion above, there are specific considerations about the institutions involved in the collaboration. Both partners need to develop a clear understanding of these issues, because a neglect of the differences in "style" between your institutions will have an adverse effect on the collaboration at some point in the future. This is particularly the case in terms of paying close attention to potential and actual differences in political power, both within and between institutions. There needs to be open-ended discussion about several issues of institutional style:

- *At what level are both of you situated in your institutions?* There is nothing wrong if a high-ranking academic collaborates with someone of low rank at his or her institution. But any equivocation, conflation, or masking of these differences likely leads to difficulty. "Lecturers," for example, are very different positions within U.K. versus U.S. institutions, and one from the latter should not parlay that title into a relationship at a college in the former.

- *What are the reporting structures for your institutions?* Each member of a collaboration may be required to inform superiors of the project at different times. A prospective collaboration can be jeopardized in situations where the project is underreported or overreported. This happens in two ways: within normalized structures or in the absence of formalized reporting structures. If there is to be institutional buy-in and support of the project, then each partner should agree to a coordinated process to bring higher-level faculty and staff into the collaboration conversation.

- *What are the expectations in-class for teacher–learner interactions?* Are "students" seen as "learners"? How is their initiative viewed? Must they attend class sessions? All of these questions require negotiation and diplomacy between members of a collaboration. The answers may vary widely within the departmental or disciplinary silos of an institution, but even more so across institutions. The pedagogy most suited to collaborative networked teaching and learning is more "learner centered" than some teachers may be used to. There might be an important issue around whether a student may ask a teacher a question or whether students should primarily be listeners.

- *What are the expectations for assessments?* As with the point above, there can be a great deal of difference in how learning is assessed. The existence of homework or assignments may be a matter of compromise or outright difference between class groups. If you and your partner plan for class members to use personal time work on shared projects or prepare for in-class sessions, then these issues must have clarity that can be worked into a strategy to communicate expectations to the classes.

Extend the Innovation 2.3

G. Brooke Lester

"Learner-centered" pedagogy means: Ask not what you need to teach your subject matter; ask what your students need in order to become learners in engagement with that subject matter!

Put another way: instructors, check your privilege. Often, we instructors find it easy to list our own needs in detail (adequate light, a particular floor plan, a given weekly session schedule, certain policies, and so on). All too often, learners' needs are either thinly veiled reexpressions of our own felt needs ("They need me to see all their faces"; "They need to put their devices away and be fully present") or are dismissively lumped into moral imperatives ("They need to take school seriously"; "They need to spend less time at their jobs"). Any plan that begins with some variant on "First, we change human nature" is doomed to failure, as is any pedagogy that begins with "First, we get only the students we think we should have."

How can we divine more successfully our learners' needs? A good place to start: after registration and before the term's beginning, take an anonymous survey of your learners' prior experience of the subject matter; hopes, fears, and expectations for the class; family and work obligations; commute durations; how many hours they expect to write and study, and how many pages they expect to read; anything that might help you determine their particular strong and weak spots as learners of whom you will be asking particular performances as evidence of understanding. Find opportunities to be surprised by what your learners prove to *actually require* in order to come to the understandings that are important to you.

Team-Building Communications Styles

Communicating Effectively and Efficiently

The communications style of your collaboration is already influenced by the manner in which the partnership first found its footing. The variations from conference networking to an email response to a blog post entail a different sort of pattern of initial communication. A recent study at MIT on distance and collaboration in virtual teams found that once participants were in different buildings, even if at the same institution, they might as well be in different countries.[12] To increase the potential for the planning of effective social learning in a collaborative networked learning session, however, your communication style must shift from asynchronous and/or faceless communications toward synchronous, face-to-face online modes of communication. Not only does this stipulation prevent the possibility of

---

12. See Frank Siebdrat, Martin Hoegl, and Holger Ernst, "How to Manage Virtual Teams," *MITSloan Management Review* (1 July 2009), http://sloanreview.mit.edu/article/how-to-manage-virtual-teams/.

multitasking—which is always sensed by others, please note—but there is an even more important reason for the collaborative networked teaching team.

Here's why: in all but one of the collaborations of which I have been a member or a manager, the failed partnerships inevitably involved an unwillingness for face-to-face online communications by one or both partners. When it came time for the actual in-class collaborative learning sessions, the teachers were completely inept at modeling comfort and competency in face-to-face online communication. Some classes were staring at their teachers' backs; other classes were hearing the bodiless voice of a teacher who refused to stand within view of a camera; other classes experienced the visible and audible frustration of a teacher who could not understand the dynamics of staging a well-designed classroom layout for audio and video. Therefore, my point here is not simply about the importance of face-to-face communication online for successful planning at a distance; the very execution of any plans depends upon comfort and actual experimentation with the technologies that might be involved.

Your personal development of the intercultural competencies list above will serve the collaboration well. Although the blogosphere is asynchronous and text oriented, rather than synchronous and video oriented, some of the guidelines for successful participation in online blogs and forums can be adapted to the face-to-face environment of collaborations for teaching. Furthermore, each of these strategies will be crucial to model and repeat in the midst of your collaborative networked teaching sessions.[13]

Etiquette for Collaborative Online Communication

1. *Plan Ahead*: Thinking through your options and alternatives for how you might respond to your partner enables you to experiment to find what works best. Becoming more conscious of how your partner responds enables you to find the best strategies use for productive communications.

2. *Add, Don't Repeat*: Synchronous collaboration does not mean that communications must take the form of improv sessions (whose line is it, anyways?!). Taking time to reflect on conversations, or even taking pauses for reflection in your conversations, will allow you to become aware of what's already been said and to try to add a new dimension, or a different slant, or another perspective.

3. *Weave*: "Paraphrase" is another way of saying this. Simply repeating the other's ideas in your own words is an excellent method to show that you are invested in making the partnership work. You may find that weaving the ideas and words of your partner into your own is a useful means of confirming mutual understanding.

---

13. Adapted from Edward J. Gallagher and Stephen A. Tompkins, "Improving the Discussion Board," Lehigh University (August 2006), http://www.lehigh.edu/~indiscus/doc_guidelines.html.

4. *Measure Your Words*: Without being curt, speak with brevity and concision. Doing so will enable points 1 through 3.
5. *Address and Sign*: Find and agree upon a method or process of addressing and responding to your partner. Using each other's names regularly supports the fact that you are indeed talking directly to each other. A similar strategy will have a profound effect upon people in the classroom during the session.

Key Moments for Communication

Face-to-face communication can very well make planning processes take longer. Asynchronous communication is excellent, in some cases, for making events and plans happen quickly. Submitting to the temptation toward asynchrony must be resisted, in my opinion, in favor of planning regular contact. To get things done, both members of a collaboration must work at making sure they and all the other "right people" are in the right place at the right times. There is no substitution for coordination in this regard.

In a nutshell, these are the key times for scheduled communication along with the relevant chapters in this book:

- Creative work (chapter 3, "The Foundation"; and chapter 4, "The Content")
- Planning (chapter 5, "The Plan")
- During a session (chapter 6, "The Details")
- Debriefing (chapter 6, "The Details")

As mentioned above, I think the better tools for communication are those that are synchronous, and the best synchronous tools involve the use of live video. There was one collaboration where the two teachers were self-described "technophobes." They were interested in working together, but completely uninterested in using anything they deemed to be "technology." And so, we met via conference call and exchanged emails. After some time, their own curiosity became piqued through the use of Google Apps such as email, document collaboration, and instant messaging. At that point, the leap to using Google's "Hangouts" was just a suggestion away. These teachers did not become "power users," but they did take their time in finding ways for the technologies to become familiar, comfortable, and useful. That they began with telephone calls rather than email is instrumental, I think, in the progression toward richer synchronous communications. I am less sure of what success this pair might have had if they had worked only at the level of email.

Whatever the case may be, it is essential that you and your partner agree upon your practices for communication. Consider making a "communications covenant," not unlike creating a "learning covenant" with your students.[14] Your agreement should include essential items such as wait times for email replies, the regularity or schedule for synchronous planning meetings, the method and means for arranging meetings, and a pattern for regularized check-ins that are distinct from explicit planning sessions. There may be other considerations than these. Each of these marks points in the process of your collaboration that will ensure your success. Indeed, modeling and patterning the same sort of agreement with your classes can make the teaching experience so much more manageable!

This chapter began with a discussion of co-hosting and a classic Venn diagram. The final parts of the chapter began to explain the practical considerations for how co-hosting actually works. These considerations help to manage and organize the experience of the overlap between your class and that of your collaborator's.

---

14. For more about learning covenants, see Fred Glennon, "Promoting Freedom, Responsibility, and Learning in the Classroom: The Learning Covenant a Decade Later," *Teaching Theology and Religion* 11, no. 1 (2008): 32–41, http://web.lemoyne.edu/~glennon/Learning_Covenant_Revisited.pdf.

Chapter Response 1—*G. Brooke Lester*
Facilitating Virtual Community

Community: it's the thing we all know we're supposed to cultivate and preserve. Community in the classroom. Communities of inquiry. At seminary, perhaps worshiping communities. Instructors who doubt the possibility of "community" in digitally mediated learning, and instructors who testify to its experience, talk past one another across a seemingly intractable demilitarized zone of differing presuppositions.

But what is a "community"? How do we know if some body of individuals can be said to experience "community" with one another? What are the constituent elements of "community," and how do we recognize them when they occur? In this chapter, Loewen describes the guest–host/host–guest relationship in terms of "mutual respect, generosity, and reciprocity." I would like to explore a commensurable and overlapping trinity out of my own experience, one derived from the work at Infed.org on sociological aspects of community: Acceptance, Reciprocity, and Trustworthiness.[15]

There, the Infed authors first describe community in terms of Place, Interest, and Communion. Community of Place is easiest to understand, perhaps. I live in the "community" of central Evanston, Illinois. At the same time, this aspect of community proves less important, or at least more complicated, on inspection. Almost all my neighbors own their homes, but I rent. Few are associated with the university campus, where I spend most of my time. The overwhelming majority I don't personally, and those whom I do, I know on account of some shared interests: we walk our dogs or our children are in the local school together. That is, while we share Community of Place, what brings us together is Community of Interest. And, of course, communities of interest extend beyond geography (e.g., costume-playing comic-book fans, birdwatchers, even Cubs fans, since that group includes die-hard expats). Students taking a course together in Hebrew Bible or world religions are part of a larger community of interest. In principle—and we do our best—the course might accomplish for some of these students (in the words of the Infed authors) "a profound meeting or encounter" amongst the learners themselves and between them and the subject matter. That is, we may experience not only "community," but Communion. When educators question whether and how "community" happens in a learning environment, we appear to mean, not geographic community, but something like "Communities of Interest that tend toward Communion."

---

15. "What Is Community?," http://infed.org/mobi/community/.

Among the "norms and habits" of community (per the Infed authors) are Tolerance, Reciprocity, and Trust. For my part, I prefer "acceptance" to "tolerance" (the latter sounding to my ear rather grudging), and "trustworthiness" as the active flipside of the experience of "trust." Acceptance, Reciprocity, and Trust ("There's an ART to Community," in the words of former student). If I want to know whether we have facilitated the possibility of "community" in a digitally mediated learning environment, I will need to discover whether learners report the experience of being accepted by others, of enjoying reciprocity with others, and of encountering trustworthiness in others.

Acceptance

Readers who have encountered the emerging phenomenon of the "unconference" may know this fundamental dictum of Open Space Technology:

"1. Whoever comes is the right people."[16]
This is in conscious reaction to the usual "conference" mentality, according to which the "right people" are big shots around whom a passively listening audience is organized. At the unconference, what makes you the "right people" to be there is that you are *there*.

When a person is made to feel unaccepted in a social space (I'll hazard this generalization), it is because those who control that space have an established idea about what is supposed to happen there, and these controllers fear that the unwelcome person will not contribute to that goal. This brings us naturally to the second dictum of Open Space Technology and the unconference:

"2. Whatever happens is the only thing that could have."[17]
There needs to be a substantive openness about what will happen in the learning space in order for participants to extend "acceptance" to all who are present. As Loewen writes in this chapter, "'Hospitality' characterizes the attitude required for teaching via collaborative online teaching because the efforts involved in planning a collaborative session require teachers to be 'open' not only to each other other, but to whatever surprises arise from that collaboration." In the open, connectivist, distributed network of the "cMOOC," that openness to outcomes is pretty obviously encoded in the structure (or perhaps "unstructure") of the course. However, what excites me about the more circumscribed structure of Loewen's networked classrooms is what I think of as "the openness of the improv." As any viewer of improvisational comedy will recognize on reflection (though perhaps perceive as paradoxical on first consideration), "improv" takes place in a tightly controlled environment. The improv comic is not simply placed on stage and told to "be funny." (That's "stand-up.") Instead, she is given closely circumscribed bounds: "Here is your partner. You're at a bus stop. She has just lifted your wallet but her cuff is

---

16. Michelle Boule, *Mob Rule Learning: Camps, Unconferences, and Trashing the Talking Head* (Medford, NJ: CyberAge, 2011), 20.
17. Ibid.

snagged on your belt. You seek to convert her to your religion. Also present is a cop. Go." As experience shows, these bounds do not stifle creativity, but inspire it. To use a mathematical analogy, even when limited to twenty degrees of freedom (rather than 360°), the artist still enjoys an infinite number of points along that arc, with the added benefit of *direction*. In the well-organized, carefully planned space of the synchronously networked classrooms, the creativity of the improv becomes available, provided an *openness to outcomes* is overtly expressed in one's lesson plan.

Reciprocity

Not a simple marketplace swapping of goods, services, or currency, "reciprocity" (per the Infed authors) describes that trusting confidence that I can give to the community (or to a member of the community) now, knowing that the community (or some member of the community) will give to me at some later date. I would call this an asynchronous reciprocity. Citing the example of the birthday gift, Chris Sahlins calls this "generalized reciprocity."[18] Obvious classroom examples include such gifts as the right to be heard; "benefit of the doubt" when a participant misspeaks or experiences difficulty being understood; the gift of careful preparation; the gift of forgiveness for occasional lapses in preparation; and others.

Trustworthiness

For the Infed.org writers, "trust" describes one's confidence that others will deal with you in a predictable way. For example, if an instructor appears to welcome interruption in one class session, and responds irritably to it during the next, students experience a breakdown in trust: the instructor is not acting in a reliable, trustworthy way. A challenge in the open, distributed learning network (in the cMOOC or "connected learning" model) is that you just don't know what people might do from one day to the next. Some learners may enter the space without a clear idea about what's going on. "Trolls" may appear (trolls always appear). The challenge is navigable: a core group of trustworthy participants takes shape, new participants become acclimated or wander away, trolls are blocked. Nonetheless, it's a challenge.

In chapter 3 below, Loewen will introduce his guideline of "times three," whereby each networked classroom session is preceded by a preparation session and followed by a debriefing session. By demanding a well-plotted set of expectations around the planned networked class session, the instructors create the necessary grounds for *trustworthiness* in the networked space. In my experience, all of us *think* that our behavior is predictable, that we are trustworthy in that respect. (Most of us, however, would probably be surprised if we asked around.) The "times three" guideline is one of several means by which I see his approach facilitating community by engendering trustworthiness.

---

18. Chris Sahlins, *Gifts and Commodities* (London: Academic Press, 1982), 189–94.

Chapter Response II—*Christopher J. Duncanson-Hales*
Finding the Courage to Teach Dialogically

In this chapter, we are introduced to a philosophy of teaching rooted in Derrida's philosophical understanding of hospitality joined with Bakhtin's concept of dialogical expressions as a promising approach to collaborative networked teaching and learning. While the overall orientation of this book is practical, some pedagogical theory is unavoidable if we are to be effective and reflective educators. One of the great advantages of the Seminarium series is the opportunity it gives me, as a reader, to join my own reflections with those of the primary author. As I was introduced to Loewen's philosophy of teaching, I reflected on my own philosophy of teaching.

For many of us, we barely consider, let alone share, our philosophy of teaching when we are on the job market. This is not surprising given the subordinate position teaching plays to research and service in most tenure and promotion processes. For those of us who take our vocation as educators seriously, however, this type of reflection is just as, if not more, important as content or technology. Periodically revisiting our philosophy of teaching and, as I do in this response, sharing it with others is one of the ways that we keep our teaching fresh and relevant to our students.

When I first began teaching I, like many of us, adopted a student-centered model of teaching. While this approach had the advantage of being more egalitarian than the "sage on the stage," teacher-centered approach that sadly continues to dominate postsecondary teaching, it often ignores the fundamental power imbalance between teacher and students. Parker Palmer, in his text *The Courage to Teach*, develops a subject-centered model that recognizes teachers *and* students as co-investigators of the subject under study. Adding this third component to the teacher/student dynamic relativizes the power dynamic by recognizing that "True community in any context requires a transcendent third thing that holds both me and thee accountable to something beyond ourselves, a fact well known outside of education. . . . The subject-centred classroom is characterized by the fact that the third thing has a presence so real, so vivid, so vocal, that it can hold teacher and students alike accountable for what they say and do."[19]

Although teachers may have a better understanding of the subject under study, this understanding, as Bahktin reminds us, is provisional and unfinished. The provisionality of understanding, as Loewen notes, requires a classroom community of

---

19. Parker Palmer, *The Courage to Teach: Exploring the Inner Landscape of a Teacher's Life*, 10th anniversary ed. (San Francisco: Jossey-Bass, 2007), 122.

hospitality and dialogue, both within the individual classrooms and between the networked classrooms that co-host sessions. In this community of teaching and learning, teachers and students are all scholars who are co-investigating the subject being studied.

My own philosophy of teaching continues this trajectory of a community of scholars by applying Paul Ricoeur's hermeneutic arc to Ernest Boyer's model of scholarship. The three movements of Ricoeur's hermeneutic arc—preunderstanding, configuration, and praxis—correspond to the first three components of Boyer's model of scholarship—discovery, integration, and application. These corresponding movements are brought together in Boyer's fourth component, the scholarship of teaching and learning.[20]

In the first instance, Boyer's scholarship of discovery corresponds to the preunderstanding in Ricoeur's hermeneutic arc. Preunderstanding is the moment of inquisitiveness that drives the scholarship of discovery. It encompasses both the knowledge we bring as a community of scholars and the knowledge we seek in our quest for understanding. Pedagogically, preunderstanding recognizes that whereas information can be imparted, understanding is lived, as Bahktin argues, in dialogue. This dialogue is represented by the second movement of Ricoeur's arc, configuration, which corresponds to Boyer's scholarship of integration. Praxis/application reflects how we bring our understanding to bear on the world and our place in the world. It drives us back to preunderstanding, as we apply newly acquired knowledge to continually seek understanding. In the words of Boyer, praxis/application asks, "How can knowledge be responsibly applied to consequential problems? How can it be helpful to individuals as well as institutions?" And further, "Can social problems themselves define an agenda for scholarly investigation?"[21] These three movements come together in Boyer's fourth component, the scholarship of teaching and learning.

Collaborative networked teaching and learning begins with preunderstanding—what the teachers and students, as an extend community of learners, know.[22] Learning is carried forward through the dialogical moment of interaction between the teacher-scholar, the student-scholar, and the subject-scholarship. Whereas the teachers collaboratively guide the learning process, it is the dynamic of collaborative networked scholarship that integrates knowledge. For this to happen, as Loewen notes, a hospitable and respectful teaching and learning community must be developed. Such a community not only respects, but fosters, difference as central to learning. By creating common intellectual ground and stimulating active learning, the collaborative and networked scholarship of teaching and learning proposed in this chapter encourages critical and creative lifelong learning that is enriched by intellectual stimulation in the fusion of horizons of understanding between geographically disparate classrooms.

---

20. Ernest L. Boyer, *Scholarship Reconsidered: Priorities of the Professoriate* (San Francisco: Jossey-Bass, 1997).
21. Ibid., 21.
22. Ibid., 23.

Chapter 3

The Foundation

Nathan Loewen

At a Glance

Finding the right starting point is an important objective. This chapter will introduce you to a field-tested process for designing collaborative networked learning sessions.

- The iterative design process
- Using common learning objectives
- Discipline-specific versus transversal common learning objectives
- Determining common learning objectives

Collaborative Course Design

My introduction to collaborative course design involved learning the hard way. My first-ever teaching assignment was at McGill University, where I was to team-teach a course for the Faculty of Religious Studies on "The Ethics of Violence and Non-Violence." This was my co-teacher's first time, too. Although the course was set to begin in January, we set about our planning in August. We began by compiling a massive bibliography based on a list of topics we thought were relevant; then we worked through hundreds of readings to create our "best of the best" course pack.

---

*QR code URL: http://chronicle.com/blogs/profhacker/planning-a-class-with-backward-design/33625

By November, we divided the topics into a course schedule and retired to write lectures in our respective offices.

The course was a train wreck. Everything seemed to go well at first. After appearing together during the first class session in January, I or my colleague delivered lecture-based content. The first fissures began to appear when comparative questions appeared on our WebCT discussion board; did the proverbial left hand know what the right was doing? Cracks appeared when we tried to create the midterm exam, which presented the class with a Himalayan task that nearly lead to open revolt when the dismal results were posted. The remainder of the term was a combination of "staying the course" amid negotiations, improvisations, and dwindling class attendance. The process of marking the final essay and exam in April left me exhausted and in low self-esteem.

We were already contracted to team-teach the course as a summer intensive. We talked through the horrors of the semester and set about revising the course, which was offered in next year's winter and summer terms, too. During those semesters, we were able to apply lessons learned and seek out resources to make our team teaching work well for us and our classes. At Vanier College, also in Montreal, I learned even more about team teaching by participating in a networked collaborative teaching network. This chapter and the following ones will outline the collective practical wisdom that emerged from these experiences.

An Iterative Process for Collaborative Course Design

My friend's grandmother had a great motivational image hanging in her pantry. It was a paper plate with a thick line of black marker around the edges, and in the middle of the plate was written "TUIT." When asked, she explained that this was a "round tuit," to encourage her to get started on things. In my mind, there does not seem to be a linear procedure that one may follow for doing course design. Whether doing so collaboratively or individually, my and others' experience is that course design is a process rather than a procedure. This chapter therefore proposes a way of "getting a round tuit." These are the foundations for collaborative networked learning.

One very important point should be emphasized from the outset: my discussion of "course design" is not necessarily about planning an entire semester-long course. Course design comes from the technical vocabulary of pedagogy, but "session design" is just as fitting for the purposes of collaborative networked teaching and learning. Neither you nor your partner should set a goal of teaching an entire course together. To repeat, this chapter is focused on setting the foundations for collaborative course designing, which might culminate in the planning of a collaborative networked learning session. Please keep this in mind.

I must immediately insert a guideline that accompanies the point above. It is the "times-three" guideline for deep learning that has emerged from my discussions with dozens of teachers. To fully realize the potential of one collaborative networked learning session, course-design plans should include two accompanying sessions. In effect, one collaborative session "is" three sessions: (1) preparation to set up for the actual session, (2) the actual collaborative networked session, and (3) a debriefing of the actual session. More of this will be explained later, but it suffices here to explain that there needs to be a preparatory session, the actual collaborative session, and a follow-up session.

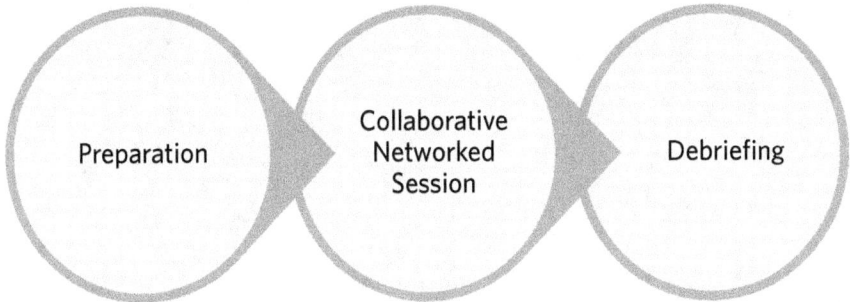

The "round tuit" imagery I hope emphasizes another point: the design process is best when done "iteratively." Working in alternating cycles of sharing–production–reflection enables a collaborative team to make several starting points and then return to them for revision. Each iteration of the planning process can then develop its detail and complexity without losing the opportunity also to make substantive revisions in order to adjust for new insights as well as unforeseen difficulties. The communications taking place throughout each iteration presents a means of getting to know collaborators. In fact, the iterative approach to collaborative work develops your skills to make on-the-fly adjustments during collaborative class sessions, too.

Here is a representation of how the iterative process works "the big picture":

The cycle of design does move in a somewhat linear fashion from unstructured beginnings through an actual session and culminates in reflective debriefing. Collaborative course design works best when the participants keep the entire cycle in mind and are able to move imaginatively to different parts of the cycle. For example, and most importantly, unstructured sharing should be returned to often in the process. The "times-three" guideline is implicitly built into the cycle, where "prepare the learners" and "debrief the session" is not only for the sake of the teachers, but to set conditions properly for the actual session and to reinforce learning outcomes. For teachers, the activities of preparation and debriefing iteratively suffuse the entire cycle alongside unstructured sharing.

Making an interactive process the foundation of course design was one lesson learned from my first experience at McGill. Everyone needs to start somewhere. We had no idea where, as both of us previously had neither taught nor co-taught.

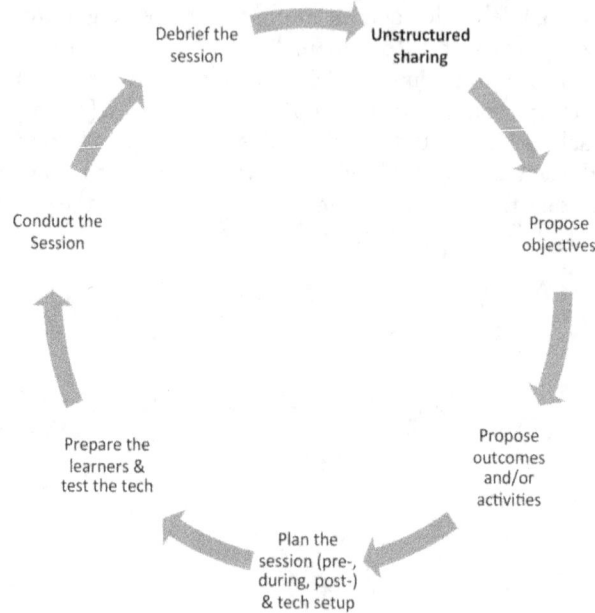

I think we were lucky to have our "train wreck" followed by an intensive May of reflection and revision. In reworking the course together we got to know each other and collaboratively built a course where we worked together. We were forced into reiteration. My future collaborations eased into the course-design process iteratively.

What Makes for an Effective and Successful Collaboration?

I will return to my first co-teaching story throughout this chapter, but that story does not address all the possible considerations for what makes for a good teaching collaboration. While there has been much published on "collaborative learning," these texts rarely if ever discuss collaborative teaching. If teachers do not actively practice and model collaboration to their learners, however, I think they are cutting short their potential insight and skills to foster collaborative learning in the classroom.

So what are the qualities of an effective and successful collaboration? How would you rank the importance of the following items? How does your ranking compare to your collaborator's ranking of these same items?

- Flexibility—with regard to the collaborative relationship as well as the effects of other things, events, or persons.
- Expectation management—to ensure similar and realistic expectations of each other and events.

- Awareness and sensitivity to cultural differences—with reference to the intercultural considerations named in chapter 2.
- Communication—where established methods and frequency of interaction are concerned.
- Responsibility and commitment—to the collaborative process and the importance of effective teaching.
- Curiosity and interest—where each of you models investment in collaboration to all the learners involved.
- Common purpose—to understand how the collaboration intersects your teaching and professional interests.
- Knowledge of divergent objectives—to clearly locate why each teacher is involved in the collaboration.
- Something(s) missing from this list?

Conducting this "poll" with yourself and your collaborator may be useful. While this is not entirely unstructured sharing, the comparison work of finding your different rankings of these items may reveal important insights for where you may take your collaboration. Each of us has different aptitudes for and attitudes toward each of the items on the list. Some may "come naturally," whereas others need cultivation.[1]

Extend the Innovation 3.1

G. Brooke Lester

One day, my administration set a challenge: What collaborative, digital projects might faculty members at my own school (Garrett-Evangelical Theological Seminary) undertake with those at another United Methodist seminary (Methodist Theological School in Ohio)? Dr. Diane Lobody proposed we consider the lines offered by Dr. Claire Potter, in a "TED Talk" video about connecting classrooms and their possibilities for more culturally diverse learning environments.[2]

Potter observes that any given institution can become only so culturally diverse. Despite efforts toward more diverse learning communities, there are always barriers: economic, geographic, and class based. Digitally mediating connections between classrooms at different institutions, schools can provide learners with an experience of diversity beyond what is possible within any one institution.

---

1. Frankly, I think all the points above are equally essential for a successful collaboration. The objective here is to initiate a productive discussion.
2. QR code URL: "Classrooms of the Future: Claire Potter at TEDxConnecticutCollege," http://youtu.be/dwqQycztc0E.

At Garrett-Evangelical, we began with a pilot attempt, wherein our "Introduction to Pastoral Care" class engaged in a semester-long set of collaborative interactions with a similar class at Methodist Theological School in Ohio (MTSO). At this pilot stage, this simply involves blending our student bodies into small Google Groups. Our plan is first to extend this program to United Methodist partners in Korea, Eastern Europe, Central and South America, and Africa. In a later stage, I would also like to see us extend the program to non-United Methodist institutions, in order to cultivate other kinds of diversity—say, by engaging a university-based Jewish studies classroom here in our own backyard at Northwestern University.

Selecting a Course for Collaborative Networked Teaching and Learning

Having a motive should not be something only for criminals. A fair presumption would be that you already have an idea of which course would benefit from interactions with learners geographically located elsewhere. Most teachers think in terms of what would be good for the class. However, a little selfishness is a good thing. Is there a different course that would create benefits for you and your teaching? Having found a partner with whom you wish to work, selecting the course should be as much about enhancing your interests as those of anyone else. There is nothing criminal about having self-motivated reasons for embarking on classroom innovation. If you lack motives for introducing collaborative networked learning into a course, then you should reconsider your situation.

There are more practical considerations for which course you might select, however. Both partners must clearly deal with these matters in order to take the collaborative process to the point of "conduct the actual session." Working through all of these considerations will allow you to create an actual calendar for potential collaborative networked learning sessions:

1. Share and review each institution's calendars. Doing so will reveal how which dates are actually possible for real-time collaborations.
   - Between which dates do the class sessions take place?
   - What are the dates of any holidays or breaks?
   - Are there any special dates? For example, are there days off for maintenance or training?
   - Are there any dates with schedule changes to compensate for any of the above? For example, is a "Friday schedule" superimposed on a Tuesday at the end of the term?
2. Share the time slots when your class sessions are run. Sharing in UTC (Coordinated Universal Time) is very useful (e.g., UTC -05:00) and it is essential to take account of any "daylight savings time" changes. International collaborations make these considerations essential, and

the non-Navajo areas of Arizona do not follow daylight savings. Knowing the precise times in UTC for your proposed collaboration will be essential if you need to make any special arrangements with either institution's registrar or IT departments.

3. Do either of your institutions or departments have specific times scheduled for major assignments or exams? Or, are there specific times that one of you wishes to set aside for this purpose?

4. What elements of your course are required or dictated by your respective departments or faculties? For example, is there a department-wide textbook or requirement for a section on specific content or competencies? And, more importantly, are these to be internally coordinated in any way? These questions importantly cover what is the "arc" or "logic" of your respective courses. If one of your courses has an idiosyncratic progression, uniquely its own, then there is an opportunity for one partner to be more flexible in scheduling the actual session(s).

5. What is the primary language for teaching and learning within your courses? If your partner's course takes place in a primary language different from yours, then you need to discuss how this may be flexible or adaptable. The actual collaborative learning session may take place using bridges for communication via images, or each group might take turns communicating in their nonprimary language, or perhaps there are competent "interpreters" in each class who could facilitate communication.

In the preparation and follow-up sessions outside the actual real-time session, you might explore the possibilities of using Web-based tools to create image-essays. For example, there are presentation platforms (such as Google Presentation[3], Prezi,[4] or Animoto[5]), and then there is the ability to create online cartoons with platforms like Bitstrip[6] or create diagrams with apps such as Google Drawing[7] and Flow Chart Maker.[8]

---

3. QR code URL: https://docs.google.com/presentation/u/0/.
4. QR code URL: http://www.Prezi.com.
5. QR code URL: http://www.Animoto.com.
6. QR code URL: http://www.Bitstrip.com.
7. QR code URL: https://support.google.com/docs/answer/177123?hl=en.
8. QR code URL: https://www.draw.io/.

These are very practical considerations that should be dealt with in the time during which the collaboration is freely discussing the possibilities for conducting actual sessions. The discussion should keep in mind the "times-three" guideline, and look for stretches of three roughly consecutive sessions that will support your in-class networked collaboration. A sense of where the collaboration could go might emerge from this work of determining the potential dates and number of in-class sessions.

At the very least, each of you should be able to share answers to these questions. Better yet, if technology permits, I would suggest creating a shared calendar. There are a myriad of platforms and means for doing so, but iCal from Apple and Google's Calendar offer two easy ways to create colorful, collaborative calendars.

Another option that I personally prefer is to use a table on a document from a word-processing application or program (e.g., Google Docs, Microsoft Word, Apple Pages, Adobe Acrobat) to create a relevant set of months. This can be very useful because these kinds of documents have commenting and review functions as well as the ability to create various kinds of formatting changes to convey meanings. For example, comments could be inserted to suggest possible dates, and red-colored bold-faced font could indicate a holiday or break. This calendar may then be completed by each partner, where access can be created through email attachments or by using a cloud-based file-storage service (e.g., Google Drive, Box, OneDrive, iCloud, Dropbox, etc.). If you choose the "email a calendar document" option, be sure to remind each other to enable the "track changes" option, so that one person's information is not lost when another writes over it (accidentally, or otherwise).

For the sake of a strong collaboration, I would highly recommend that you review the completed calendar or document over a real-time video connection. Not only will this allow for unstructured sharing, by which you may know each other better and share sudden insights; the synchronous connection will reinforce the outcome toward which your process is moving: a networked collaborative class session in real time.

Why Not Start with Content?

I'll be honest—starting with content does not work. Attempts to start collaborations based on content often begin with exchanges of information, such as:

- Textbooks
- Resources
- Syllabi
- Course outlines
- Topic or reading schedules
- Bibliographies

That conclusion derives from the experience of advising or participating within over a dozen different collaborative-teaching scenarios. The "traditional" approach to course design, for some, is established either by education providers or by institutional requirements. Textbooks are often written with the intent of shaping a teacher's course, and publishers hope that this is a selling point. Your course will be easier to teach with a textbook that organizes the content for you. Governments, institutions, or departments may require that certain content be presented in your course. The reasons may vary, for example, from confessional or ideological agendas, to demands made by industry or professional orders, or to an interest in creating equity or fairness across multiple sections of the same or similar courses. In all of these scenarios, the attempt to find places where "content" overlaps is not the best path toward successful collaboration.

There are several reasons why starting with content does not work well. One is attitudinal. Somehow, the activity of negotiating topics and resources leads to a mindset that each member of the collaboration is "making a sacrifice" in order to meet the content of the other. Oftentimes, the result is one partner disengaging or feelings of unfairness and/or resentment arising. Another related problem in starting with content has to do with power differentials. When one partner starts making claims about disciplinary expertise or categorical claims about content that must be in the course, the other begins to defer or accommodate for reasons that are not, simply put, collaborative.

Starting with content often leads the collaborators to revert to asynchronous communication. Suddenly, in my experience, the so-called partners begin sending emails or uploading folders with syllabi, schedules, bibliographies, lecture notes, and document files of various resources. Doing so defuses collaborative potential by virtue of the tacit or explicit expectation that each will thoroughly read the other's materials and somehow come to the same conclusion about the importance or admissibility of one or more items of content.

Finally, the emphasis on content misleads the collaborators into thinking very narrowly about education as the transmission of information. "Here is the information in my course," and "Here is mine." This happens as an electronic exchange in most cases, and rarely through actual real-time conversation. As a result, the collaboration begins thinking in terms of "information technology" and forgets about the importance of "communication." Any collaboration headed in this direction is not likely able to sustain the iterative process of repeatedly communicating across the phases of the constructive project. The "content mindset" in all likelihood leads the teachers to plan very static activities and goals for the learners. While this makes for a "networked learning session," it rarely makes the session collaborative. The learning amounts to reading text or watching a very poor imitation of television in real time.

Why Not Start with Technology?

Do you remember my discussion of the teachers that started out working only by telephone? They are a collaboratively networked power team, primarily because they still use the telephone to communicate. There are many hip, cool, and fascinating technologies available today. I am definitely not immune to the hype, since I literally get excited about something new each week. My interest varies from something as simple as a new mobile-device app or LCD projector configuration to complex considerations of how to facilitate collaborations across networks and IT security issues. I imagine that you likely get excited about the former kinds of developments, which seemingly have greater relevance to your teaching life.

Knowing each other's technological knowledge, abilities, and skills capacities is an important matter to begin sorting out in the process of unstructured sharing. Frank discussions along the continuum of interest or disinterest in technology are crucial. In fact, this topic should be reiterated constantly through the collaborative process, so that collaborators may share the highs and lows of their technological experience.

As mentioned in the previous section, I think it is risky to deploy technology in the classroom solely in order to convey information. Anyone along the continuum from technophile to technophobe is actually capable of successfully organizing collaborative networked learning, precisely because one key to success is not to start with the technology.

Collaborating through Common Learning Objectives

So what remains as a foundation to begin collaborative networked teaching and learning? A clear answer has emerged from my experiences as well as from all of the networks and programs that use an approach like the one explained and explored in this book: real-time discussions toward common learning objectives. A learning objective is a brief explanation of what a teacher wishes to be learned. Content and technologies are not ends in themselves; they are among the basic means by which a teacher facilitates the learner's demonstration that a learning objective is achieved. Teachers are able to collaborate successfully when they can agree upon one or more learning objectives they wish learners to accomplish. Everything else follows from there.

Stepping Backward to Move Forward on Collaborative Teaching

The approach I am suggesting to you is sometimes called "backward course design." More technically, it is a part of pedagogies related to learning by design, integrated design, and constructive or pedagogical alignment.

 L. Dee Fink discusses integrated design in his book (*Creating Significant Learning Experiences: An Integrated Approach to Designing College Courses*[9]) and at the QR code to the left.[10]

 Mark Morton at the University of Waterloo provides several resources for "backward course design" using his "triple alignment" method.[11]

I call this approach "backward" only vis-à-vis the "traditional" methods of course design noted at the beginning of the chapter. For teachers who are used to starting with content first, starting instead with learning objectives seems "backward." I personally think that the designations are the inverse!

Defining Common Learning Objectives

The iterative process is facilitated by arriving at common learning objectives. Every step of the iterative course-design process must be able to engage with common learning objectives, just as every step of the iterative process must be capable of unstructured sharing that engages the other steps of the process. The potential for pedagogical insight is thereby amplified.

I sincerely believe that, had I known this, my first team-taught course at McGill would have avoided disaster. We made it to the end of the course without imploding on each other, largely because there was good will and good faith on the part of both my colleague and me, along with plenty of amateur pluck. I am sure that other teaching collaborations can survive for the same reasons, but this does not make them effective or successful at teaching.

Other teaching teams, outlined briefly above, literally did not complete their actual in-class collaborative networked learning sessions. In one case, the planned seventy-five-minute, real-time session lasted for twenty-two minutes. Those partners chose to cancel all their future sessions. Another case saw all the planned sessions take place, but one of the teachers chose to remain almost completely

---

9. L. Dee Fink, *Creating Significant Learning Experiences: An Integrated Approach to Designing College Courses* (San Francisco: Jossey-Bass, 2003).
10. QR code URL: http://ideaedu.org/sites/default/files/Idea_Paper_42.pdf.
11. QR code URL: https://uwaterloo.ca/centre-for-teaching-excellence/sites/ca.centre-for-teaching-excellence/files/uploads/files/302.pdf.

silent through all the sessions. In both of these cases, the collaborators vigorously resisted the proposal to settle on common learning objectives rather than on content.

Strategies for Creating Common Learning Objectives

In order to arrive at common learning objectives, each collaborator must spend some time doing personal reflection on the following questions about your respective courses:

- What big ideas are addressed in my course?
- Which accessible questions may lead learners to inquire about these big ideas?[12]
- By the end of my course, what should my class be able to do? (Note the emphasis on "the class.")

These questions are meant to take you into the general and overall logic and purpose of your teaching and classroom learning. The last question in particular is about collaborative learning outcomes. Sometimes this question is not considered by teachers, textbooks, departments, institutions, and governments. Nevertheless, learners will be working with others throughout their lives. Knowing what you want your class to do together will provide a pathway for thinking about what two classes might do together in a networked environment.

Extend the Innovation 3.2

G. Brooke Lester

When Grant Wiggins and Jay McTighe invite instructors to consider what "big ideas" animate their approach to the subject matter, they ask this in service to a particular approach to course design: Understanding by Design.[13] When creating or revising our course (as here, in response to Nathan's invitation to networked classrooms), it's our habit to begin with our usual resources and activities. We think that these are "the course," when they are, rather, the deck chairs that we rearrange while the ship goes . . . somewhere (forward? in circles? downward?). From a UbD perspective, we begin instead (Stage One)

---

12. Adapted from Grant P. Wiggins and Jay McTighe, *Understanding by Design Professional Development Workbook* (Alexandria, VA: Association for Supervision and Curriculum Development, 2004), 13.
13. Grant P. Wiggins and Jay McTighe, *Understanding by Design*, exp. 2d ed. (Alexandria, VA: Association for Supervision and Curriculum Development, 2005).

with the big ideas or "enduring understandings" that we want our learners to engage, crafting them into "essential questions" that open up the subject matter and invite the generation of further questions and open-ended inquiry. "What is 'the good life'?" "What is religion?" "Where does religion fit in political activity?" "Does a person choose a religion, or vice versa?"

In Stage Two, we ask, "What performances would a learner need to accomplish in order to demonstrate successful engagement with this unit's enduring understandings?" *These are not yet activities or projects.* For example, "The learner should *interpret* two texts that make competing claims about God," or "the learner should *apply* an analytical approach learned in class to a case study." Only in Stage Three does the instructor choose the resources and activities that will prepare students to accomplish these desired performances.

The following additional questions take you further into the substance of your respective courses. If you can identify sections or units of your courses, reflect upon and determine your responses to the following questions:

- What key skill(s) should a learner acquire in this unit?
- What should learners be able to do with the skill(s)?[14]

If both collaborators are willing and able to formulate answers to these questions, then they have the beginnings of a strong foundation for collaborative networked teaching and learning. These answers can lead toward the discussion about what goals, activities, and assessments are suitable for the actual collaborative class session. In that discussion, you should explicitly avoid sharing about specific content. You should engage in unstructured sharing that leads away from citations and footnotes and leads toward finding what is stimulating and interesting in your teaching and learning. Then, you should ask each other about what your teaching has in common:

- Big ideas?
- Big questions?
- Collaborative learning outcomes?
- Individual learning outcomes?
- Important skills?
- Actions or productions based on skill(s)?

---

14. Ibid, 14.

Extend the Innovation 3.3

Christopher J. Duncanson-Hales

While Loewen suggests that you think about "big ideas" after you have found a collaborative partner, I think it is even better to add this step to your self-reflective inventory in preparation for finding the right collaborative match. Carefully reflecting on and naming these big ideas, and only then exploring networks and resources that collaborative partners may share or even challenge, contributes to developing a dynamic and engaging networked session. A successful collaborative partnership and networked teaching and learning session configures these big ideas with those of our students to create new knowledge. Epistemologically, it is through this movement that new ideas emerge; however, it is only in the moment of reflection/praxis through debriefing where these big ideas can flow back into preparation informed by these new "pre-/postunderstandings." The whole iterative process begins with our own reflection on big ideas.

Once you have arrived at one or more commonalities, you must ask: How many course hours are each of us willing to spend on what we hold in common? The answer to this question may help you determine how many sessions you wish to allocate to the creation and actualization of collaborative networked teaching and learning.

What If We Still Do Not Have Anything in Common?

I am a collaborative teaching idealist who believes that ANY teacher from ANY discipline is able to collaborate with ANY other teachers. Ideally speaking, for example, a physics or computer-aided-design teacher should be able to find points of commonality with a religious-studies teacher. Here are two strategies that may "grease the wheels," so to speak.

Plan A: What Are Your Discipline-Specific Learning Objectives?

Zoom into the specifics, rather than considering big ideas and general skills. Each collaborator should exhaustively determine the learning objectives for his or her course. At this point, you may begin discussing matters of knowledge.

- What, specifically, should learners know by the end of your course?
- What are learners supposed to do at the end of your course? In other words, list the kinds of evaluations used and the specific questions or demands made by those evaluations.

Plan B: When All Else Fails, Select Transversal Learning Objectives

Transversal learning objectives name certain kinds of general education learning outcomes that are expected to be transferred by the college experience. At their most basic, these objectives articulate expectations of a certain level of literacy, numeracy, knowledge, and skills. They sometimes include "soft skills," which are expectations for a certain level of aptitude for productive socialization. Your institution may or may not have a general education element across its curricula and programs. Your institution may or may not have student services, which often offers programming that seeks to establish certain transversal outcomes.

Transversal learning objectives are truly discipline-agnostic. They may be expected in the context of any disciplinary or departmental context. What are they, specifically? Review the "benefits for teachers" and "benefits for learners" outlined in chapter 1, above. These lists articulate transversal attitudes, aptitudes, and skills that are, in my mind, essential expectations for the completion of a college-level education.

So "Plan B" is quite simple: (1) Review the benefits of collaborative networked teaching and learning with your partner. (2) Select which of these benefits you can agree upon to create a learning experience for your class. (3) Formulate them as a learning objective: "by the end of our collaboration, our students will be able to . . ."

Reaching Common Ground/Next Steps

My objective for this chapter has been for you and your partner to find the right starting point for designing your collaborative networked learning session. You can literally start anywhere. I am serious! You could begin by "cold calling" another classroom by Skype and improvising your way through fifteen minutes, or seventy-five minutes, of a "learning session." Some starting points are more successful and effective than others, however. Starting with content or technology has potential, but also definite limitations. The following two chapters will focus on moving from learning objectives toward what is traditionally thought of as "content." Technology, the means of delivering the actual course design, will only be discussed in the final sections of the book.

I wanted to introduce you to a field-tested process for designing collaborative networked learning sessions, where teachers embark on the iterative process of course design by agreeing upon shared learning objectives. The following chapters will ask you to keep those objectives in mind, returning to these objectives repeatedly. Course design done well is an iterative process, largely because teachers need to maintain a grasp of the whole while working discretely with the parts therein. Alongside a good dose of unstructured sharing, the iteration and reiteration of common learning objectives is of highest importance in a collaborative teaching context.

Chapter Response I— *G. Brooke Lester*
Preparing for a Cross-Cultural Classroom Experience

Back in chapter 2, Nathan Loewen expresses a goal that, by networked classrooms, we create conditions for students to undergo a cross-cultural experience. Here in chapter 3, preparations are underway to facilitate that experience.

In biblical studies, we often encourage our learners to see reading the Bible as a kind of cross-cultural experience. Toward that end, we sometimes help students to come to better understanding of their own social standpoint through the use of the "Student Self-Inventory on Biblical Hermeneutics," often simply called the "Gottwald Self-Inventory" since it first appeared (with its history) in an essay by Norman K. Gottwald.[15] The self-inventory was developed for Christian seminary students taking a course in biblical studies.

Here, I offer a substantively revised version of the self-inventory, tailored for the broader subject matter of the college or university religion department. Most of the words in the list below are direct quotations from the Gottwald Self-Inventory. But I have revised it liberally, changing from a Christian-centric inventory of biblical hermeneutics to a more general inventory of religious self-understanding and practice.

How might a university-based, religious-studies classroom use Gottwald's self-inventory to prepare for a cross-cultural educational experience with a partner classroom from another context? I recommend that the instructor create an anonymous survey that produces tabulated results available to the participants (easily accomplished with a "survey" tool in one's Learning Management System or on the Web). Viewing and discussing the tabulated results, the students can some to a more self-aware, data-informed sense of where they are (so to speak) as a group. In this way, the student body can (before engaging their networked partners) better understand themselves as occupying particular, overlapping spaces on a much larger, variegated, intercultural religious terrain.

---

15. Norman K. Gottwald, "Framing Biblical Interpretation at New York Theological Seminary: A Student Self-Inventory on Biblical Hermeneutics," in *Reading from This Place, Vol. 1: Social Location and Biblical Interpretation in the United States*, ed. Fernando F. Segovia and Mary Ann Tolbert (Minneapolis: Fortress Press, 1995), 251–61.

The Revised Self-Inventory

1. *Church History/Tradition*: What is my institutional (church, synagogue, mosque, etc.) history and tradition regarding interpretation of authoritative texts (the Christian Bible, Jewish Scriptures, Qur'an, etc.) in religious life . . . if any?
2. *Authoritative Criteria*: What are the norms or standards (beyond authoritative texts) recognized in my tradition? These may include a founder of the tradition, a worshiping body, a confession, a creed, a set of customs or practices, a type of personal experience, a social commitment, as well as other possibilities.
3. *Working Theology*: What is my actual working theology regarding the interpretation of authoritative texts and other religious practices? To what extent is this the same or different from the official position of my religious institution or the "average" viewpoint among my institution's associates?
4. *Ethnicity*: How does my ethnic history, culture, and consciousness influence my interpretation of authoritative texts and other religious practices?
5. *Gender*: How does my gender history, culture, and consciousness influence my interpretation of authoritative texts and other religious practices?
6. *Social Class*: How does my social-class history, culture, and consciousness influence my interpretation of authoritative texts and other religious practices? Since the dominant ideology in our society tends to deny that social classes exist among us, or to belittle the significance of class, it may take considerable effort on your part to identify your class location. For starters, you can ask about work experience, inherited wealth, income, education, types of reading, news sources consulted, social and career aspirations, and so on, and you can ask these questions about yourself, your parents, your grandparents, your associates, your neighborhood, your church.
7. *Education*: How does my level and type of education influence my interpretation of authoritative texts and other religious practices? If I have had technical or professional training in nonreligious fields, what impact does this have on my interpretations and practices? How does my age and "generation" affect my experience of interpretations and practices?
8. *Community Priorities*: Does my religious institution have a vision of the common good of the community in which it is located? Does it have any explicit commitments to the attainment of the common good?

How does my institution's view of its relationship to the larger community influence my interpretations and other religious practices?

9. *Explicit Political Position*: How does my avowed political position influence my interpretation of authoritative texts and other religious practices? Politics is about as narrowly conceived in this country as is class. The term "political position" in this question refers to more than political party affiliation or location on a left–right political spectrum. It also takes into account how much impact one feels from society and government on one's own life and how much responsibility one takes for society and government, and in what concrete ways. Also involved is how one's immediate community/church is oriented toward sociopolitical awareness.

10. *Implicit Political Stance*: Even if I am not very political in the usual sense, or consider myself neutral toward or "above" politics, how does this "nonpolitical" attitude and stance influence my interpretation of authoritative texts and other religious practices? What is the implicit political stance of my church and of other religious people with whom I associate?

11. *Attitude toward Other Faith Traditions*: What is my view of the relationship between my faith and those of others (Christian, Jewish, Muslim, Hindu, other, humanist, or other atheist)? To what extent is my view informed by direct experience of other religious communities?

12. *Customary Exposures to Authoritative Texts*: How does the mix of uses of authoritative texts to which I have been or am culturally exposed influence my interpretation of authoritative texts and other religious practices? Such uses may include worship, preaching, religious instruction, private study, ethical and theological resourcing, solitary or group devotions or spiritual exercises, and so on.

13. *Text Translation*: How do the translations of authoritative texts and study materials that I use influence my interpretations and other religious practices? What translation(s) do I regularly or frequently use, and why? What line of interpretation is expressed in them? Do I accept these without question or do I consult other resources of information to compare with them?

14. *Published Resources*: How do the published resources I regularly or sometimes consult influence my interpretation of authoritative texts and other religious practices? Among these resources may be one's private library, a church or seminary library, periodicals, religious educational materials, sermon helps, and so on.

15. *Intent and Effect of Proclamation*: How do my religious leaders (or I myself) understand the role of authoritative texts in preaching, and

how does that understanding influence my own pattern of interpretations and other religious practices?

16. *Orientation to Scholarship*: Are the categories and terminology of academic religious scholarship completely new to me, or do I have some familiarity with them? How does my attitude toward and use or non-use of academic religious scholarship influence my interpretations and other religious practices? Am I inclined automatically to accept or to reject whatever an academic religious scholar claims? Does the academic religious scholarship I am familiar with increase or decrease my sense of competence and satisfaction in the study of authoritative texts?

17. *Family Influence*: What was the characteristic view of authoritative texts in my childhood home? Have I stayed in continuity with that view? Do I now see authoritative texts rather differently than my parents did (or do)? If there have been major changes in my view of authoritative texts, how did these come about? How do I feel about differences in biblical understanding within my current family setting?

18. *Life Crises*: Have I experienced crises in my life in which authoritative texts or religious practices were a resource, or in which I came to a deeper or different understanding of authoritative texts or religious practices than I had held before? If so, what has been the lasting effect of the crisis on my interpretations and other religious practices?

19. *Spirituality or Divine Guidance*: What has been my experience of the role of authoritative texts in spiritual awareness or guidance from the divine? What biblical language and images play a part in my spiritual awareness and practice? How do I relate this "spiritual" use of authoritative texts to other ways of reading and interpreting authoritative texts? Do these different approaches to authoritative texts combine comfortably for me or are they in tension or even open conflict?

Chapter Response II—*Christopher J. Duncanson-Hales*
Considering Learning Disabilities in Collaborative Learning Environments

Nathan Loewen introduces us to a process for collaborative course design, beginning with his reflections on the challenges he encountered with his first collaborative teaching experience. As one who is a relatively new teacher, I can relate with the learning required in one's approach to pedagogical formation. Indeed, as mentioned in chapter 1, one of the great strengths I see in his pedagogical approach is the opportunity it allows for mentorship among faculty from diverse institutional, and perhaps disciplinary, perspectives.

Loewen takes a risk in beginning a chapter on course design by describing his first teaching experience as "a train wreck," a risk that I believe is warranted as it highlights what, for many of us, was an inadequate pedagogical formation based on replicating what are often the poor teaching habits of senior faculty. As I stated in an article I wrote for a local student interest magazine, "The reality is, unlike secondary school teachers, university faculty are not rewarded for inspired teaching. While faculty are released from teaching to pursue their research, they are never released from research to pursue teaching. Only service and research, not teaching, lead to tenure and promotion." Despite this, many of us seek opportunities to develop and improve our teaching, both for the sake of our students, and, as I discussed in the previous chapter, for the sake of our scholarship.

It was this sense of seeking pedagogical resources to inspire my own teaching that I found Nathan's proposed "backward course design" most appealing. This process, based on "pedagogies related to learning by design, integrated design, constructive or pedagogical alignment," challenges us as educators to go beyond the syllabus and the extrinsic value of the mere passing on of information to taking seriously the intrinsic value of iterate course design rooted in the dialogical and dialectic process of developing shared learning goals and . . . collaborative networked learning.

With that said, I would like to bring into sharper focus one of the strengths implicit in this approach, which is the need for course design not only to "quote" but also to take into account increasing recognition of diverse learning and teaching styles, and the necessity, sometimes mandated by legislation, to accommodate learning disabilities among students and, increasingly (if quietly), many faculty. On this latter point, I have often commented that matriculation with a PhD is a sure-fire cure for a learning disability.

Ministry of Training, Colleges and Universities (MTCU)[16]

Statistics compiled for 2006–2007 by the College Committee on Disability Issues:

- Students with learning disabilities made up 40.8 percent of students served by the offices for students with disabilities at Colleges of Applied Arts and Technology in Ontario.
- Students with learning disabilities represented 4.8 percent of the total number of college students.

2007–2008 statistics from MTCU (from Colleges and Universities Year-End Reports)

- College students with learning disabilities (LDs): 7,785 (10.1% increase over 5 years).
- University students with LDs: 5,546 (17.9% increase over 5 years).
- Total postsecondary students with LDs: 13,331 (13.2% increase over 5 years).
- Total postsecondary students with LDs or attention deficit hyperactivity disorder (ADHD): 16,551.
- Students with LDs made up 2.24 percent of the total student population.
- Students with LDs or ADHD made up 2.78 percent of the total student population.

While LDs are well documented throughout the general population, including undergraduate and graduate students, for what I can only surmise is fear of being professionally stigmatized for a perceived intellectual weakness, LDs are conspicuously absent from the ranks of most university teaching faculties. One approach that complements Nathan's backward course design and allows a certain amount of anonymity to avoid stigma, both for students and faculty, is Universal Instructional Design (UID).

Principles of Universal Instructional Design

The term Universal Design (UD) was coined in the early 1970s by Ronald Mace, the founder of the Center for Universal Design at North Carolina State University (NCSU). This movement in architectural design "asserted that designers have a responsibility to proactively consider human diversity in the design of public

---

16. Learning Disabilities Association of Ontario, *Learning Disability Statistics*, http://www.ldao.ca/introduction-to-ldsadhd/ldsadhs-in-depth/articles/about-lds/learning-disabilities-statistics/.

spaces so that resulting environments and products are useable by the intended audience: the diverse public."[17]

University of Guelph's handbook: *Universal Instructional Design (UID): A Workbook for Faculty Teaching at a Distance.*[18]

As applied to course design, the principles of Universal Instructional Design levels the instructional playing field so that the widest range of students, with or without cognitive or physical disabilities, are able to engage fully in the scholarship of learning. This inclusivity builds flexibility into the instructional design and development of educational materials through seven principles identified by the University of Guelph. The following list provides a summary of some examples of UID elements that are easily adaptable to a collaborative networked learning environment.[19]

1. Accessible and Fair (Equitable) Use

    All students should ideally use the same means to fulfill course requirements—identical if possible, equivalent when not. Instruction should be designed to be useful and accessible by people with different abilities, respectful of diversity, and with high expectations for all students.

    a. Design of Learning—using Web-based courses with online resources so students can access materials in electronic formats as needed.

    b. Design of Environments—using accessibility checkers on Websites.

2. Flexibility in Use, Participation, and Presentation

    Learning is most effective when it is *multimodal*—when material is presented in multiple forms, and when students have multiple means of accessing and interacting with material and demonstrating their knowledge (being evaluated). Instruction is designed to meet the needs of a broad range of learner preferences. Students can interact regularly with the instructor and their peers.

    a. Design of Learning

    - designing resources so they can be reused in a number of ways (e.g., in class, online)

---

17. Sally S. Scott, Joan M. McGuire, and Stan F. Shaw, "Universal Design for Instruction," *Remedial & Special Education* 24, no. 6 (November 2003): 369–79. Available from Academic Search Elite, Ipswich, MA.
18. QR code URL: https://www.uoguelph.ca/tss/uid/uid-workbook-DE.pdf
19. Adapted from the University of Guelph's Webpage on "Universal Instructional Design Principles" at http://www.uoguelph.ca/tss/uid/uidprinciples.cfm.

- providing choice in assignment topics, formats, and due dates when possible
- using online discussion, and group work to foster peer-to-peer learning
- posting exercises and quizzes on a website that students use outside of class to learn on their own

  b. Delivery Strategies
  - presenting information using a variety of media: text, graphics, audio, and video
  - using a variety of strategies during lecture such as discussion or problem solving

3. Straightforward and Consistent

   Instruction is designed in a clear and straightforward manner, consistent with user expectations. Tools are intuitive. Unnecessary complexity or distractions that may detract from the learning material or tasks are reduced or eliminated.

   a. Design of Learning
   - ensuring course content, assessment, and learning objectives are all consistent
   - designing activities or assignments to minimize noncritical tasks (e.g., avoiding the need to learn nonessential software so that students can begin learning immediately
   - applying grading standards consistently across students and assignments

   b. Delivery Strategies
   - structuring class time in a consistent manner
   - differentiating between essential and supplementary information

   c. Design of Materials or Tools
   - organizing information on a Web page or manual in a manner that makes it easy to navigate
   - structuring and formatting material for easy readability
   - testing new technology resources for usability

4. Information Is Explicitly Presented and Readily Perceived

   Course expectations are transparent. Instructions are easy to understand. Communication is clear. Any barriers to receiving or understanding are removed. Information may be presented in multiple forms.

a. Design of Learning
- providing SMART (specific, measurable, achievable, relevant, and timely) learning objectives
- making expectations and instructions about assignments explicit
- providing a grading scheme or rubric along with examples
- providing policies, procedures, and expectations in the course outline

b. Delivery Strategies
- facing the class and making eye contact when speaking
- using tools such as a microphone, PowerPoint, etc., in class to ensure that information is communicated effectively

c. Design of Materials or Tools
- providing lecture outlines online that students can annotate during class
- creating digital forms of hard-copy materials
- using ALT (alternate text) tags for any images on Web pages so that these may be identified by screen reading programs used by text-only browsers or students with disabilities

5. Supportive Learning Environment

Instruction anticipates that students will make mistakes. While instruction recognizes that errors are necessary, and if handled properly, present powerful learning opportunities, it tries to minimize hazards that can lead to irreversible errors and failures. Instruction also recognizes that systems will fail and things can go wrong—thus, a tolerance for error and preparation by way of backup are important so that learning will not be interrupted.

a. Design of Learning
- breaking large assignments into components so that students can receive formative feedback to minimize or correct errors
- providing frequent opportunities for assessment and feedback during a semester
- providing a list of frequently asked questions about an assignment
- using online quizzes or tutorials that provide a safe environment to identify weaknesses
- providing students with ample time for online work in case of system failure

b. Design of Materials or Tools—ensuring that software provides feedback when a user makes an inappropriate selection

c. Design of Environment—implementing safety procedures in labs so that unintended actions do not have catastrophic effects (e.g., injury)

6. Minimize or Eliminate Unnecessary Physical Effort or Requirements

Instruction is designed to minimize *nonessential* physical effort (i.e., not related to a learning outcome) in order to allow maximum attention to learning.

a. Design of Learning—allow the use of a word processor whenever possible for submissions

b. Delivery Strategies

- placing reserve materials online so students do not need to physically travel to a library
- allowing assignments to be submitted electronically

7. Learning Space Accommodates Both Students and Methods

The learning space is accessible and the environment supports multiple instruction strategies.

a. Design of Environments

- in small classes, using circular seating arrangements during discussion to allow students to see one another's faces
- providing enough left-handed seats

While each of these principles is implicitly integrated in this and the following chapter, it is nevertheless important that they be explicitly named in order to create as diverse a teaching and learning environment as possible. By beginning with developing shared learning goals, for instance, rather than content or technology, Loewen encourages the development of a supportive community of learners and a collaborative instructional learning environment that is sensitive to the diversity of learners and instructors. The principle of straightforwardness and consistency corresponds with his "keep-it-simple" principle. The principle of equitable use corresponds with the need to recognize and account for the challenges of imbalances in technologies between classrooms and among students, and to the need to choose technologies and software programs that are intuitive to use and require minimal technical know-how.

In the context of a collaborative networked teaching and learning environment, backward course design informed by the principles of universal instructional design has a final and, I would argue, critical role in addressing the imbalances that can arise in the variety of approaches to accommodating—or not accommodating—learning disabilities in postsecondary institutions.

> **Key Points of Accessible Fair (Equitable) Use**
> - Flexibility in use, participation, and presentation
> - Straightforward and consistent
> - Information is explicitly presented and readily perceived
> - Supportive learning environment
> - Minimize or eliminate unnecessary physical effort or requirements
> - Learning space accommodates both students and methods

While increasingly learning disabilities are for the most part, if sometime reluctantly, accommodated in North American and Western European postsecondary education, the same cannot be said for some of the educational partners we may encounter in a collaborative teaching and learning network. Designing courses and collaborative networked sessions using the principles of UID has the potential to overcome these imbalances by building "accommodations" into the development of the course itself. In this way, as is the case with designing a building where wheelchair accessible ramps blend into the overall design and décor of a building, accommodations for LDs are integrated into the landscape of the course without drawing specific attention or stigma to those who need them.

Chapter 4

The Content

Nathan Loewen

At a Glance

Effective social learning is at the center of collaborative networked learning. This chapter is focused on how you and your partner can generate suitable goals and activities for these sessions.

- Relating common learning objectives to goals and activities
- Creating collaborative learning goals
- Generating collaborative learning activities
- Evaluating learning activities

Moving from Learning Objectives to Session Goals and Activities

A former, younger version of myself was a self-employed bicycle mechanic. I paid my way through college by toiling away in the rearward recesses of big-box stores, assembling bikes and repairing the most heinously crooked wheels that clearly had been subjected to adolescent abandon. The process of "truing" a wheel requires patient attention to the whole and the parts. Each spoke is related to the others, and so the art of big-box-store bicycle maintenance is an iterative process of doing

---

*QR code URL: http://seminariumblog.org/books/student-centered-teacher-centered-pedagogy-oh/

evaluation, adjustment, intervention, eyeballing, measuring, and applying experienced intuition. Here is the punchline of the vignette: I cannot imagine what it would be like to true a wheel collaboratively!

Creating learning experiences is not unlike truing wheels. Keen attention to the whole and the parts, simultaneously, must always be given throughout the process. The previous chapter explained how the course-design process is described as "iterative," or circular rather than linear. If this is true, then collaborative course design can and sometimes does become overly complicated. This is why the previous chapter proposed laying a foundation for your collaborative partnership that works with the iterative process. In my experience, arriving at common learning objectives and allowing them to suffuse the planning process is the clearest route toward collaborative course design.

Carts and Horses: Learning Objectives and Learning Goals

In the previous chapter, I asked you to set aside content and technology in favor of learning objectives. I think that doing otherwise puts the proverbial cart ahead of the horse. The "horse" for your collaboration needs to be a learning objective that can pull your pedagogical cart through the planning process toward the actualization of your collaborative networked learning session. I will leave the analogy's extension up for interpretation, saving to say that the "learning goals" yoke the pedagogical cart to the objective(s).

"Cart Before the Horse" (Best and Worst Ever Photo Blog). Public domain.

You might wonder what the difference is between "goals" and "objectives." The distinction is parsed out in the language of course design. The former makes a more specified step toward the actual teaching session, where the latter creates the horizon for planning one or more sessions. A learning goal is a succinct statement of what the teacher wishes for the students to *do*. By working out learning goals, teachers are able to articulate one or more specific actions to which they may then connect a demonstration or production. Doing so is meant to establish transparency and good communication in the classroom, since learners are clearly informed about what is expected of them.

When teachers collaborate to create a session, the movement from learning objectives to learning goals is a way to provide a movement toward the practical matters of teaching. When a collaboration begins with content, teachers almost immediately must begin negotiating differences of interpretation regarding specific authors or concepts in their field or discipline. The point of this approach is not to elide or subsume those very real professional differences. The point is very much to have those differences emerge in the context of demonstrating skills and actions toward the creation of academic productions. In the best-case scenarios, teachers can plan for learners who can then see those differences emerge in context.

Making learning goals the next step in the process also helps mark a clear progression toward creating collaborative assignments. Articulating the learning goals will make it possible to explain answers to most of your learners' questions: What skills must they demonstrate? What knowledge is required for them to use these skills? And, perhaps most importantly from a learner's perspective, how will I be evaluated? And this takes place without having to already be discussing the assignments themselves. Likewise, the use of technology will start to emerge later in the process in a situation where the collaborating teachers already possess fundamental agreements on what they wish to do together.

During the actual collaborative networked learning session, if you state the learning goals, everyone involved will be able to locate themselves within the same "cart" being pulled by clearly identifiable "horses." The learning goals will help you show the connections between the learners' activities and the collaborative networked learning session; they very well may demonstrate connections with your respective courses, too. You will be able to show these connections from the preparatory activities through the actual session and toward the assignments or evaluations that you have designed with the learning goals in mind.

Creating Workable Learning Goals

A workable learning goal should speak clearly to your particular group of learners by asking them to demonstrate a specific skill or action vis-à-vis a specific context. In a collaborative networked teaching scenario, doing so entails communication between the teachers that establishes a clear sense of each other's learners. With a sense of who is your collaborative "class," it is possible to start aiming learning goals at, or just above, their collective level of expected aptitude and mastery. The question of context is partly solved because the sessions will be held in an online environment, but the question remains open when you and your partner think about how learning from the session may be applied in the future, be it in the summative evaluations for your courses or in some future context.

Finding the right words for learning goals can be difficult, but the job is made much easier by refering to Bloom's taxonomy. In 1956, Benjamin Bloom proposed this categorization of kinds of learning into educational objectives ordered into domains by virtue of their relative complexity. Much later, a "revised version" emerged, which can be accessed interactively at Iowa State University's Center for Excellence in Teaching and Learning at the top QR code. The second QR code is a non-Flash verion that works on iOS devices.

Robert Marzano provides another set of terminology in response to Bloom's taxonomy. Marzano's book, *A New Taxonomy of Educational Objectives* (2000) presents a different approach to understanding how knowledge and learning are organized. The last QR code is a document that provides Marzano's taxonomy.[1]

Here is an example of what happened with two teachers who embarked upon a collaborative networked teaching project. After reviewing coordination questions such as those outlined in chapter 3, they agreed to create six in-class sessions. Then came the conundrum: How do we do this? One course was an ethics course for the sciences, and the other was a general education course in social issues. The geo-social differences between the classes were vast, where an urban group of roughly forty specialized learners, largely from the medical sciences, was going to collaborate with a rural group with learners from a variety of programs. The solution was to agree on several specialized and transversal learning objectives:

1. To situate significant ethical issues in Canadian society.
2. To organize ethical questions and their implications into coherent patterns.
3. To debate the ethical issues with peers.
4. To communicate and collaborate with other learners at a distance in real time.
5. To master the use of ICTs in an academic environment.

---

1. QR code URLs: (1) http://www.celt.iastate.edu/teaching-resources/effective-practice/revised-blooms-taxonomy/; (2) http://www.celt.iastate.edu/teaching-resources/effective-practice/revised-blooms-taxonomy/blooms-model-text/; and (3) http://wiki.adams50.org/mediawiki/images/f/f9/Bprtc_Marzano_taxonomy_verbs.pdf

From this point, the teachers were able to start generating more specific learning goals that related these broader objectives into the actual learning sessions which they hoped to plan. The iterative process is embodied in the successive level of detail or specificity that is added to the goals:

1. To situate significant ethical issues in Canadian society
    1.1. Identify a significant ethical issue
    1.2. Describe what is morally significant about the issue
    1.3. Articulate a personal point of view on the issue
2. To organize ethical questions and their implications into coherent patterns
    2.1. Apply the basic elements of a moral theory and its terminology to an ethical issue
    2.2. Identify the principal elements of a moral argument
    2.3. Analyze the implications of the issue using a moral theory
3. To debate the ethical issues with peers
    3.1. Identify the ethical aspects of a controversial issue
    3.2. Apply a moral theory to the issue
    3.3. Determine an outcome that is consistent with a moral theory
    3.4. Compare different possible outcomes of different moral theories applied to the same issue
4. To communicate and collaborate with other learners at a distance in real time
    4.1. Master the basics of online conversation
    4.2. Create online documents with others at a distance
5. To master the use of ICTs in an academic environment
    5.1. Master the basics of online word processing
    5.2. Master the basics of creating an online presentation
    5.3. Make an online presentation to others at a distance

Once this list was created, the organization of the six sessions began to fall into place. The teachers could iteratively return to this basic list and determine whether their creative direction was on course. Furthermore, at the beginning of the term, the teachers took the time to introduce each other's classes in the context of explaining the learning objective and the learning goals. Their classes were then clearly informed, and frankly quite excited, about the learning experiences that were upcoming in the semester. The learners could also clearly draw connections for themselves between these "special classes" and the overall structure of their courses. Instead of apprehension and skepticism, a general air of excitement and anticipation emerged as both classes were looking forward to two things: (1) the unexpected interactions with their colleagues at a distance and (2) learning in a collaborative networked context.

In the example above, the collaborating teachers were able to begin articulating the next steps in their planning. Activities could be designed for preparation, in-class sessions, and assignments. Content could be arranged with respect to the activities and the kinds of knowledge that the teachers knew would be necessary for their learners to demonstrate their fulfillment of the learning goals. Connections could be made with larger summative evaluations at the end of the semester.

Extend the Innovation 4.1

G. Brooke Lester

It is a truth universally acknowledged, that an instructor in possession of a good learning goal must be in want of some verbs.

Look again, if you would, at Loewen's list. Look at the verbs. "Identify . . . describe . . . articulate . . . apply . . . determine . . . compare . . . create . . ." An instructor, let's say by means of an "Understanding by Design" approach to course design or revision, has settled upon some "enduring understandings" and "essential questions" that she means for her learners to engage. For example, in Loewen's networked collaboration between an ethics-for-sciences course and a general education social-issues course, she might raise such essential questions as "How do we identify moral issues at stake in a quandary?" Or, "Does ethical argument seek to illuminate issues or persuade interlocutors?" Now, looking for performances by which learners can offer incontrovertible evidence of engagement, she needs . . . verbs.

Loewen's resources on Bloom's taxonomy will provide some verbs associated with that taxonomy's primary action words (recall, understand, apply, analyze, evaluate, create). A Web search will generate additional lists of verbs: for example, "analyze" further suggests "distinguish, categorize, estimate, compare," and so forth. For example, see Mia Macmeekin, "Bloom's Revised Taxonomy with Verbs!" at the QR code to the left.[2]

Finally, *Understanding by Design* breaks "understanding" into "Six Facets" that themselves each suggest a sheaf of action words; the Facets are explanation, interpretation, application, perspective, empathy, and self-knowledge.[3]

Creating a useable learning goal does not emerge spontaneously out of thin air. Sometimes there is difficult conceptual reflection and evaluation required of the teachers. Starting with learning objectives, the big ideas, is useful. But the learning goals should lead toward the next step: How will the learners prove that they accomplished the learning goal and have retained the skills and knowledge to do so? The articulation of the learning goals feed into thinking about assignments and the issue of tracking student progress.

---

2. QR code URL: http://anethicalisland.wordpress.com/2014/06/05/blooms-revised-taxonomy-with-verbs/.
3. Grant P. Wiggins and Jay McTighe, *Understanding by Design*, exp. 2d ed. (Alexandria, VA: Association for Supervision and Curriculum Development, 2005).

The learning goals in the example above might seem mundane or simple. And they are purposefully stated in the simplest terms possible. This is because the principle of K.I.S.S. is very useful in teaching: "Keep it simple, stupid." The slogan comes from Alcoholics Anonymous, where it is used to keep the immediate situation in mind. By focusing on the smaller steps, it is less likely that one meets a wall. And it is more likely that one can count up the victories and accomplishments happening in each moment. Such is the case for teachers and students as much as it is in dealing with addiction. Simple and incremental progressions under the horizon of the big idea(s) prevents walls from emerging in the course-design process, and ultimately prevents conceptual "jumps" that are difficult for learners to grasp.

Evaluating Your Learning Goals

Prior to thinking about whether or not a learning goal is useful for collaborative networked teaching and learning, there is another important and basic test. Ask the following question: Is your learning goal simply a topic? A learning goal may seem "elegant" or "simple" if it states something like "to read Derrida's *Gift of Death*" or "to study the Trinity." If the learning goal merely states a topic, it gives the learners very little understanding of what they are expected to do, produce, and know. Even worse, the teacher is setting up an impossible task for the very same reason. Simply stating a topic does not create the pedagogical grounds for a teacher to know who is being taught to do what, what the learners ought to know, the sort of scenario or context in which learners might find themselves knowing and doing, and finally, what level or degree of competency should be demonstrated by the learners. Creating a learning goal useful for collaborative networked teaching and learning is identical to the above!

Therefore, generally speaking, a useful learning goal should lead toward an explanation of the following:

- Identify the learners
- Establish the learning context
- Articulate learning expectations
- Determine the level of competency

You and your partner may take this evaluation of your learning goals much further by putting them to the following test.

1. Does the goal describe what must be (a) learned, and (b) done? Answering this question will grant learners an important indication of what you think will be "new" or added to their knowledge and abilities.
2. Are you asking learners to do something that is feasible, visible, and measurable? As noted earlier, any step that is too great becomes a wall, and learners will either give up or cheat out of frustration with the barrier. You can outline reasonable expectations by using verbs for

specific actions whereby learners may demonstrate their competency. As a result, both you and they will know when a learning goal is unmet, achieved, or outrightly surpassed!

3. Is the learning goal clearly understandable for your audience? Remember, your class likely has less background knowledge and expertise than you!

4. Is the learning goal "terminal"? That is, do learners need to be guided through other distinct, supporting goals embedded within the learning goal? More often than not during the iterative planning process, you will create a learning goal that has other goals loaded within it. You do yourself and your learners a service by unpacking these discrete actions, skills, and knowledge. Revising your learning goals or tracing out the subgoals will help learners make sense of your expectations.

5. Does the learning goal have an application? The goal must make practical sense to you and your class, and so the goal should point toward some kind of connection to the overall course and possibly beyond the course itself. The former may be indicated by a clear link to an evaluation, and the latter by virtue of a readily understandable connection to learners' programs or occupational futures.

A more detailed look into Robert Noyd's approach may be found in his online manual, "A Primer on Writing Effective Learning-Centered Course Goals."[4]

Creating Activites from Your Goals

One emphasis of this chapter is to emphasize the importance of moving from learning objectives toward learning goals. The process should be done in real-time discussions with your collaborator(s). This creates maximal conditions for creativity, because the variations in perspective and knowledge of learners will produce a well-rounded articulation of the learning goals. The other emphasis of the chapter is to help you move from the learning goals toward the articulation of what sorts of activities may best enable your classes to accomplish your stated goals.

Pre- and Postsession Activities

The kinds of activities that you create should keep in mind the "times-three" guideline from chapter 3. That is, you should be planning two supporting class sessions

---

4. QR code URL: http://www.designlearning.org/wp-content/uploads/2010/03/Writing-Good-Learning-Goals-by-Robert-Noyd-US-Air-Force-Academy.pdf.

for each in-class collaborative networked learning session. The guideline should be applied as a guide and not as a rule; and so, while spending an entire class session prior and afterward is unnecessary, there should be clear and detailed consideration about how the pre- and postsessions help prepare learners for the actual session as well as help learners extract confirmations of their new knowledge and skills from the actual session. Therefore, class activities encompass preparation, the actual session, and follow-up.

Preparatory activities are there to support the in-class session. They may address particular learning goals and subgoals, with an eye toward ensuring that learners are prepared to engage each other. The preparatory activities might actually involve prior interactions. These activities range from asking the classes to read through instructions to having them formulate and explain their knowledge or positions prior to the engagement with another activity. For example, the following list of preparatory activites have been done in collaborative networked sessions that I know of (there may be many more possibilities!).

There are functionality-related preparatory activities to ensure access to the planned-for technologies and platforms, such as:

- Confirming operations of online platforms (e.g., sending a test message)
- Registering for online platforms (e.g., setting up a Moodle account)
- Submitting username or account information (e.g., a Gmail profile)

And, not unrelated to the above suggestions, there are content-related preparatory activities that involve the successful usage of those platforms and technologies, such as:

- Confirming that instructions have been read
- Circulating an agenda for the in-class session
- Requesting a text be read (e.g., a Website, blog, or chapter)
- Making introductions to a class or small group
- Uploading an image or video (e.g., an avatar or thirty-second "hello" video)
- Responding to a text (e.g., on a discussion forum or blog)
- Proposing a topical question (e.g., also on a discussion forum or blog)
- Collecting and uploading data, image(s), sound(s), video(s), or text
- Posting a map (e.g., on a map Website or within an LMS)
- Posting a work of prose
- Uploading a research essay or discussion article
- And, possibly most important: asking for help or clarification of any aspect of the in-class session

Follow-up activities also support the in-class session. These should be explained or revealed to the classes in the preparatory stage, so that they have a clear idea of the direction of their learning. Following up the actual session may take either summative or formative form, and the follow-up may take the form of an evaluation or simply a no-stakes registration of participation. Summative evaluations are rarely sensible follow-up activities for collaborative networked learning sessions. The events of the actual session will likely have a high degree of unpredictability, and the learners' experiences of the events in the session will likely be highly varied, too. As a result, a summative evaluation that places the weight of high-stakes marks on the session normally leads to a mixture of paralysis and frustration.

Extend the Innovation 4.2

G. Brooke Lester

Something there is that doesn't love *a surprise*.

Which is darkly convicting, when you consider how frequently an instructor will foist surprises off on his students while bending heaven and earth to avoid the possibility of any surprises actually breaking out during sessions. Loewen here (as also in chapter 2) urges the instructor to "explain or reveal" follow-up plans to students back in the preparatory stages; having "a clear idea of the direction," the learners are comfortable enough that conditions are right for the "high degree of unpredictability" that characterizes genuine "dis-covery" and "un-covering" new understandings, and not just uninspired "cover-age" of content.[5]

Learning, understood here as the *making* of meaning, is in this sense a *creative* act . . . and nothing kills creativity like fear and uncertainty. Bringing learners "into the plan" takes the fear of surprise off of their shoulders, and generates conditions for *you* to be surprised in that always unpredictable space where learning is constructed.[6]

The list of preparatory activities above is a good set of examples for follow-up activities, too, with the exception of the request to confirm functionality. Follow-up activities may include an added element of formative evaluation, which may take the form of peer review or small-group work. In scenarios where groups or individuals are required to produce an outcome outside of the class session, it only makes sense that these productions should be reviewed and discussed in a subsequent in-class collaborative networked session. Otherwise, the accountability to others at a distance is diminished.

---

5. Wiggins and McTighe, *Understanding by Design*, 352–53.
6. Readers who want to hear more about creativity, the removal of fear, and the "open mode" necessary to creative work should search the Web for a video of John Cleese's lecture "How to Inspire Creativity" (yes, *that* John Cleese). The video can be hard to find, but a transcript is available here: "Lecture on Creativity," http://news.genius.com/John-cleese-lecture-on-creativity-annotated.

In-Class Activities for Collaborative Networked Teaching and Learning

You and your collaborating teacher are the ones who ultimately decide which specific activities would best suit your learning goals. It may be a challenge to align the learning goals and the actual activities that are hatched by your combined creative powers. This is why the planning process is described as "iterative." Even though you have ideally begun as this book advises, laying your collaborative foundation with the learning objective(s), your planning process should always iteratively return to earlier decisions in order to verify the accuracy of your intentions. It could very well be the case that you agree upon an adjustment of the learning objective or learning goals at a later point in the planning process. The most important point here is that you do so together with a strong consensus that an alteration of objective(s) and goal(s) is necessary. Completing this sort of revision is not a "bad thing." The value of iteratively maintaining alignments among the elements of your session design will be realized during the interactions with the participating classes. The potential to engage your learners fully is partly dependent upon the clarity with which they perceive the connections among the stated objective(s), goals, and activities.

For collaborative learning experiences, the issue at hand is focused by a concern to plan activities that facilitate interactions with other students. Including transversal learning goals in your list is useful in this regard, since transversal goals often involve interdisciplinary and so-called soft skills. Where possible, you and your partner should specify what is the "interaction" and what are the "appropriate skills" related to that interaction. For example:

- Free-form discussion
- Structured discussion
- Questioning and answering
- Peer learning
- Skill sharing or instruction
- Laboratory observation or discussion
- Demonstration
- Presentation
- Games or gaming
- Problem solving
- Case study
- Some other form of group work

Keep in mind that the above list is about general forms of activities that you set into a collaborative networked environment. In nearly every context and wherever possible, the intent should be to have learners interact with others at a distance. As noted in the "benefits for students" in chapter 1, activities that establish relations among remote peers is a completely different context from that of in-class peer activity. Your learners will be working with others in the same location in most situations, but that is not a compromise. A different kind of interaction emerges among learners who are both invested in communicating and working with other learners at a distance; new perspectives and approaches will emerge among learners in each class as they attempt to meet the learning goals that you have communicated.

Peer-to-peer interactions in the collaborative networked environment may encourage the following kinds of peer learning:

- Identify misunderstandings or missing information
- Participate in the practice of providing and acting upon peer evaluation
- Examine each others' work for errors (so long as the activity focuses on one aspect at a time!)
- Reflect on personal or academic transformation
- Observe progress toward learning goals
- Encourage and/or inform others toward achieving learning goals

Collaborative activities often work best when they go beyond academics to include the affective and psycho-motor dimensions. What this means, in the work of L. Dee Fink's research on learning, is that the desire and motivation to learn increases when there is evidence that personal investment will be constructive in that learning endeavor.[7] In Fink's opinion, this is missing from Bloom's taxonomy. For Fink, this means that learners should be given the opportunity not only to discover and apply new knowledge and skills; there should also be the opportunity for making connections with learners' lives outside academia; learning about themselves and others; developing and evaluating their feelings, interests, or values; and drawing upon these to find how they might become better learners. The nature of the collaborative networked environment provides plenty of opportunities for learners to develop new perspectives, practice empathy, and increase their self-knowledge.

Indeed, there is a related reason why the iterative process described in chapter 3 includes "unstructured sharing" and an emphasis on the iterative process. The benefits for teachers go beyond professional and academic development. If the teachers do not engender some kind of affective attachment to their work on collaborative networked teaching, then the learners will certainly have difficulty "feeling it," too. The emphasis on real-time video in the planning process also testifies to the importance of psycho-motor involvement. Seeing and hearing each other within the planning process leads to higher levels of investment and increased transparency in communication. By paying attention to how the collaboration relationship is developed in these discussions, teachers may get a sense of how to structure in-class

---

7. See L. Dee Fink, *Creating Significant Learning Experiences: An Integrated Approach to Designing College Courses* (San Francisco: Jossey-Bass, 2003).

activities that promote collaboration amongst their learners. Doing so increases the potential that learners will come to see themselves in a new way, act differently on the basis of their new knowledge and/or skills, and actually find out that they may care more about or value something that can motivate their studies.

And so the discussion of possible in-class activities should keep the above in mind while considering the structuring of activities such as the following:

- Group bonding/ice-breakers
- Topical activation/engagement
- Learner reporting/input
- Dialogue to acquire new information, perspectives, ideas
- Reflection on a common topic
- Questioning
- Formulating and/or solving problems
- Analyzing, comparing, and/or evaluating findings, outcomes, or solutions
- Sharing results
- Determining prior knowledge
- Reflection on new learning

At the City University of Hong Kong, there is a free online primer in "Outcomes Based Teaching and Learning and Constructive Alignment." Following the entire MOOC is very useful for professional development, but the most interesting part for this chapter is the Teaching and Assessment Ideas Tool.[8] By simply selecting from the various drop-down menus, you can start generating ideas for activities, tasks, and assessments alongside related action verbs.

Evaluating Your Activity

A collaborative networked teaching and learning session may have only one or perhaps several activities. Please note that there is no expectation that each learning goal or subgoal ought to have a corresponding activity that singularly serves that goal. In actuality, several activities may be associated with several goals. You may

---

8. QR code URLs: (1) http://www.cityu.edu.hk/edge/obtl/elearn_tool/index.htm; and (2) http://www.cityu.edu.hk/edge/obtl/elearn_tool/tool.htm.

even find it the case that every activity in a class session affirms or accomplishes all of the learning goals set out to be accomplished. Each activity may accomplish a part or whole of a goal. In fact, deeper learning outcomes are derived from a learning experience that includes engagements of learning goals on multiple occasions.

All of this is to say that learning goals should be experienced iteratively. You may find it helpful to draw up a line-by-line listing of activities that correspond to each learning goal. Alternatively, in a process of reflection and unstructured sharing, a spontaneous or brainstormed set of activities might be generated by a collaborative teaching team. Once such a list has been created, it is useful to cross-check that list with the learning goals that were set forth for the session. Going line by line, collaborating teachers may then associate all or none of their goals with each item on the activity list. There may be a justification for keeping an activity that "scores low" on the number of associated learning goals; for example, perhaps an activity is thought to be useful in activating learners' interest in the session, and the scope and depth of the sessions' engagement with the learning goals will emerge in further activities. Indeed, this is where a team's understanding of themselves and their learning context is useful to make judgments about how the collaborative networked session ought to unfold.

In the example referred to in the earlier parts of this chapter, the collaborating teachers drew up a list of activities that they hoped would correspond to a session plan. Their idea was to present their classes with a case study of an actual event: the expropriation of lands and homes by the Canadian government to create a national park. With one class from a rural college and the other from an urban context, the teachers hoped that this topic would generate a sufficient level of difference in the perspectives of their two classes. After some unstructured sharing and deliberation, this was their list of proposed activities:

- Independent class sessions introducing two moral theories
- Short sharing session on who has visited a national park; opportunities for short descriptions
- Co-review the Parks Canada website for their explanation of national parks
- Watch a short music video about the destruction of villages
- A virtual guest who lived in one of the villages reviews her parents' "eviction" letter
- Unstructured Q&A of the virtual guest by the classes
- Small-group application of one moral theory to the case
- Discussion as a whole of small-group findings

Taking their list of learning goals and list of activities side by side, the teachers were able to work through whether or not their proposed set of activities adequately engaged their learning goals. What they found was that the first four items on their list were very much focused on setting up the scenario for the engagement of their learning goals. Their decision to independently introduce the theoretical background for the session fulfilled the "times-three" guideline, which expects that at least one class session is required to prepare learners adequately for a productive collaborative networked session. The last four activities turned out to emphasize highly their second and third learning goals: "to organize ethical questions and their implications into coherent patterns," and "to debate the ethical issues with peers." The latter goal did not amount to an actual debate-format class session. Rather, "debate" was taken in a looser sense of becoming able to situate the competing and controversial aspects of an ethical issue. The former goal very much depended upon the effectiveness of the first four suggested activities, which were meant to provide sufficient background knowledge and context for the learners to gain the insights required to accomplish learning goals two and three. The last two learning goals, concerned with online communication and academics, benefited from the addition of a virtual guest and the expectation that learners would work in virtual teams for their analysis of the ethical issue.

It is worthwhile to make particular note of how the proposed list of activities suggests the use of online tools and communication technologies, but the listed activities do not give specific details. The teachers wisely left that issue for later stages in their planning process. Their task in the short term was simply to generate a list of activities and cross-reference it with their learning goals.

Beyond whether an activity adequately engages your learning goal(s), there are some basic questions that should be asked of any proposed activity:

1. Does the activity help learners prepare for future assignments?
2. Will the activity engage the personal interests of the learners?
3. Does the activity require learners to *apply* and *do* something?
4. Will learners perceive the activity as feasible?
5. Is there alignment between the supporting and primary activities?
6. Is there sufficient time and resources for the activity to be completed in class?
7. Does the activity lead toward the creation of a virtual production or demonstration?
8. Will the activity compel learners to work collaboratively?
9. Does the class know how their activity will be assessed?

Hitching the Cart

Proceeding from learning objectives to the creation of learning goals and activities is the focus of the iterative course-design process. By working in circles, much the way a bicycle mechanic straightens a wheel, you and your partner must collaborate around the learning objective(s) to create a balanced set of activities that will support the weight of the learning expected of your classes. The development of a solid set of activities owes as much to making time for creating reflection as it does to moving incrementally toward specific details. Through this phase of the process, the issue of "technology" should be suspended, since this concern threatens to "put the cart before the horse." Those practical matters will emerge in the course of the following chapter, where the actual session plan is put into place. What matters in this chapter has been to establish the "content" of a collaborative networked learning session through the progression from the foundational learning objectives. Hopefully, during the actual session, everyone involved will be able to locate themselves within the same "cart" being pulled by clearly identifiable "horses," where your teaching team's learning goals connect the learners' activities with your collaborative interests and expectations.

What Happened Between the Rural and Urban Classes?

The teachers in this chapter's example anticipated that their classes' different geo-social and cultural contexts would create a productive exchange during the collaborative networked session. And it did. At the beginning of the term, they had conducted intercultural attitude surveys to establish a baseline for another survey after their collaborative networked class sessions (approved by their institutions' research ethics review boards). The results of the second survey were disheartening upon first look: the urban class specifically expressed greater distrust of "rural people," while the rural class results were unchanged. Upon reflection, the teachers agreed that the first survey registered their optimism, and the second registered more honest opinions. A key contributing factor, in the teachers' opinion, was that the real-time nature of the actual class session provided unexpected opportunities to both air and discuss stereotypes. The rural class was unsurprised about the presumptions and naïveté expressed by the urban class, of whom several argued for the great yield of utility in displacing "a few farmers and fishermen" for the benefit of "so many others." Similar expressions from the rural learners, such as "they were there before you," were not welcomed by the urban learners. Big ethical questions about immigration and indigenous peoples needed to be unpacked by both teachers in subsequent class sessions. The teachers concluded that an opportunity for further research was clearly being presented to them, and that they had definitely created an intercultural learning experience that may not have been possible using a serial, pen-pal connection between their classes.

The Content

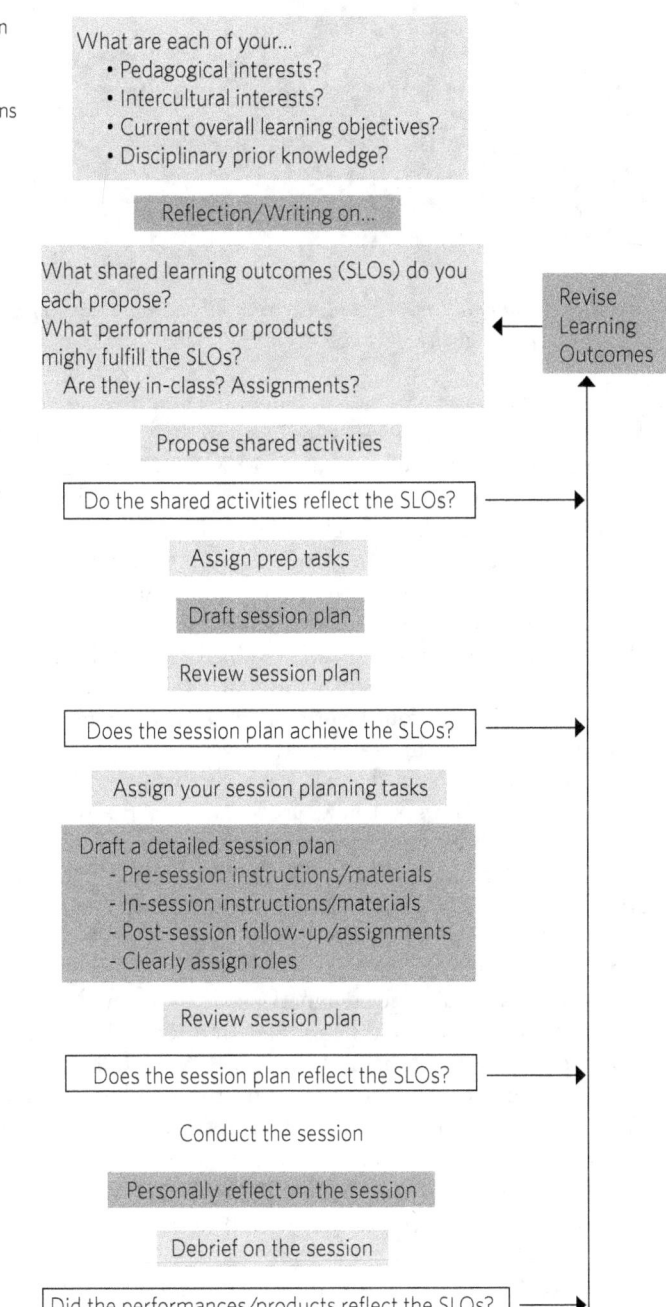

The figure illustrates how, according to the approach explained in this chapter, the planning process always returns to the learning goal(s).

Chapter Response I—*G. Brooke Lester*
Teaching Online: The Bad News, the Worse News, and What to Do about It

> *I'm yummy all right, but please try a nibble, not #bite. I'm just not ready to be a zombie tonight. #dodge #TvsZ*

So wrote @savasavasava, as she fought for her life over a weekend of "Twitter vs. Zombies."[9] The organizers simply wanted an occasion for learners to embody a "lightning-fast version of a connectivist MOOC," to "build a community" of real-time game developers, "learn more robust ways to use Twitter." What broke loose is the kind of happy heck made possible when novel learning environments prompt us to summon the courage to loosen our grip *even a bit* on our habitual classroom activities, and ask: "Okay . . . what do I want to happen in the learner? Forget the 'what?'. What is the 'why'?"

We all have activities to which we return again and again in our course designs. And it's natural to ask, when undertaking networked or other online teaching, "How will I do [insert your favorite activity here] online?" The bad news—always ask for the bad news first—the bad news is that maybe you can, but there are innumerable ways to skin that cat, each involving that thing you're trying so hard to avoid: *change*. The good news is, the way to the solution is through a question *always* worth bringing to our habitual resources and activities: "*Why* do I do this?" From an Understanding-by-Design perspective, "How does this activity allow learners to demonstrate compelling evidence of such enduring understandings as I wish them to have developed? Or how does it prepare them to demonstrate such evidence in later performances?"[10]

Let's say that you've gotten good results with in-class debates in the past. In your model, students would be assigned into opposing teams, undergo a research period, and enjoy some dedicated class time to fashioning arguments (perhaps exchanging these in some form). In a final session, the two teams would participate in a structured debate: opening statements, taking questions from a moderator or from one another, responding and rebutting, and making closing statements. Obviously, this is unlikely to work well in the limited time of a networked class session, to say nothing of a completely asynchronous course or unit. But, on reflection, the

---

9. "Twitter Vs. Zombies: New Media Literacy & the Virtual Flash Mob," Pete Rorabaugh and Jesse Stommel, founders of Hybrid Pedagogy: http://www.jessestommel.com/blog/files/twitter_vs_zombies .html. For Hybrid Pedagogy, see http://www.hybridpedagogy.com/.
10. Wiggins and McTighe, *Understanding by Design*, 146–71.

instructor might decide that the networked session (lending itself, if desired, to rapid back-and-forth, interruption, sudden turns) might be a terrific venue for the teams to debrief or "postmortem" a debate already accomplished asynchronously (say, over a week's time, using a discussion forum or Google Docs). It's a pretty big change. In one sense, it's no longer "your" debate activity. But the point is not to preserve "your" activity; rather, it is to provide learners an analogous opportunity to accomplish performances giving evidence of understanding, or to prepare for such performances coming later in the course.

Similarly, you may have a habit of including "fishbowl" discussions.[11] In this format, a small inner circle carries the main phase of discussion, while an outer circle listens (with or without a backchannel by which to communicate with one another silently); in some forms, an outer-circle member may join the inner circle, at which point one member of the inner circle must retire to the outer circle. If you ask, "How will this work in a networked session?," the answer is, "Who knows?" You may call one class the "inner" circle and the other the "outer," or you may combine a few members of each class into a single inner-circle team. Some aspects of your original structure may survive (for example, a Twitter backchannel for the outer circle), but some won't (like a literal, physical circle for participants). So ask yourself: *Why* do I like the fishbowl? How does it permit learners to demonstrate convincing evidence of the enduring understandings animating this course, or enable them to accomplish such performances later? Exploring the "why?" will tell you what kinds of revision will accomplish what you hope for your learners.

Like a writer, though, an educator has to be ready to "kill her darlings." (This is the worse news! But don't worry, it's all still fine. Have a chocolate.) When translating your favorite activities into a networked classroom or other digitally mediated learning space, stand back from time to time and look: Has this plan turned into a Rube Goldberg machine, employing umbrellas, kitchen sinks, and manual typewriters just to cage a mouse? Keep returning to your learning goals. If what you love about the debate activity is that learners are forced to patiently and generously engage alternative points of view, then can they do something instead that involves critical appraisal of a political op-ed? If the big payoff of the fishbowl is for highly motivated volunteers to have a discussion unencumbered by underprepared peers, then maybe something similar can be accomplished with small teams pointed toward specific areas of some larger social problem or quandary.

> "How do I do [insert my favorite activity] in a networked classroom, or an online class, or a hybrid certification program, or . . . ?" Ask yourself "Why?" And consider killing your darlings. With any luck, they'll rise again. Mind the zombies! #dodge #TvsZ

---

11. A search-engine inquiry will yield any number of excellent versions of a "fishbowl discussion/conversation."

Chapter Response II— *Christopher J. Duncanson-Hales*
International Experiential Learning

With the analogy of putting the cart before the horse in this chapter, Loewen presents a further refinement of backwards course design by introducing learning goals and objectives to the overall design of a course. Workable learning goals, he argues, "should speak clearly to your particular group of learners by asking them to demonstrate a specific skill or action vis-à-vis a specific context."

Loewen points out, the "question of context is partly solved because the sessions will be held in an online environment, but the question remains open when you and your partner think about how learning from the session may be applied in the future, be it in the summative evaluations for your courses or in some future context." It is this "future context" as presented in the chapter's rural/urban classroom example that piqued my interest, not so much as presented, but as a "big idea," suggesting an application of collaborative networked teaching and learning as a tool for international experiential learning (IEL) programs.

As Loewen notes, the teachers in the example anticipated their classes' different geo-social and cultural contexts, anticipating that these difference would "create a productive exchange during the collaborative network session." The results of pre- and postsession surveys revealed what to the instructors was a surprising result of the urban class expressing a greater distrust of "rural people." The real-time nature of the collaborative sessions, they concluded, "provided unexpected opportunities to both air and discuss stereotypes." The diverse local context of each of the classes, brought together in the global context of a collaborative network teaching and learning environment surfaced "Big ethical questions about immigration and indigenous peoples [that] needed to be unpacked by both teachers in subsequent class sessions."

As this example shows, collaborative networked teaching and learning has the capacity to surface big ethical questions beyond the localized the specific geo-social and cultural contexts of the networked classrooms. As postsecondary institutions respond to globalization and the pressure toward internationalization and "global harmonization of higher education policies and programs," increased attention is being given to establishing "global citizenship" as a key graduate attribute gained from postsecondary education. One need only review the international program offerings of North American universities for evidence of this trend.

 Dalhousie University's overview of their experiential learning program.[12]

 Simon Fraser University's experiential learning program includes coursework at partner institutions.[13]

Shelane Jorgenson and Lynette Shultz note that the development of these attributes in graduates takes place over the course of an entire undergraduate and/or graduate education and "therefore require connecting learning beyond particular courses, programs and even disciplines."[14] They go on to note that one of the principal means by which transdisciplinary learning to prepare global citizens is accomplished is through experiential learning and study-abroad programs. It is this transdisciplinary learning through international experiential learning (IEL) that is key "to preparing citizens to address the complex global issues and interconnectedness of life in our highly globalized world,"[15] and where collaborative networked teaching and learning can make a positive contribution.

Rebecca Tiessen traces the development of experiential learning through the popularization of the work of David Kolb who, with Ron Fry, developed the experiential learning model (ELM). ELM "focused on experience, observation of—and reflection on—that experience, understanding abstract concepts based on that reflection, the testing of new concepts, followed by repetition of the process."[16] The modern iteration of IEL began in North America in the 1950s with the establishment of work-study and year-abroad programs. With the increased attention paid to internationalization and globalization these programs began to expand and were included as part of academic programs and, in some cases, requirements for graduation. Building on the early work of Kolb, IEL programs include an international focus requiring travel and cross-cultural experience. Tiessen favors the term "international experiential learning" over other commonly used terms like "work study"

---

12. QR code URL: http://www.dal.ca/academics/programs/undergraduate/commerce/what_will_I_learn/coop_work_terms.html.
13. QR code: http://www.sfu.ca/students/calendar/2013/summer/international-experiential-learning/intl-exper-learning-cert.html.
14. Shelane Jorgenson and Lynette Shultz, "Global Citizenship Education (GCE) in Post-Secondary Institutions: What Is Protected and What Is Hidden under the Umbrella of GCE?," *Journal of Global Citizenship & Equity Education* 2, no. 1 (Special Edition, 2012): 3.
15. Ibid.
16. Rebecca Tiessen and Robert Lee Huish, "International Experiential Learning and Global Citizenship," in *Globetrotting or Global Citizenship? Perils and Potential of International Experiential Learning*, Rebecca Tiessen and Robert Lee Huish, eds. (Toronto: University of Toronto Press, 2014), 5.

and "year abroad," as it is a "comprehensive term that encompasses the practical, ethical and theoretical components of the learning/volunteer abroad experience."[17]

One of the key ethical issues the IEL shares with collaborative networked teaching and learning is, as Tiessen notes, the "use of communities in Canada and the Global South as extension of classroom spaces."[18] Tiessen goes on to recognize that although "we have much to learn from people and organizations committed to social and/or global justice, we much also be careful not to treat communities in the Global South as laboratories for testing an academic or career choice,"[19] concluding that effective experiential learning that is aware "of the ethical impacts of international experiential learning must also contribute to a transformative learning which is grounded in the struggles for equality and justice and facilitate the creation of 'authentic allies'. International experiential learning programs therefore provide a valuable opportunity for reflecting on how much we need to learn about the world around us and the importance of global competency for good citizenship."[20]

A significant challenge faced in creating authentic allies is the intercultural preparation and postexperience debriefing and integration of the cross-cultural experience. Julie Drolet goes so far as to define attention to predeparture and postexperience preparation as an ethical imperative, identifying the following five components that IEL must pay attention to:

1. Building and sustaining international field partnerships and relationships
2. Developing mutually agreed-upon learning arrangements
3. Supporting language acquisition and cultural preparation before departure
4. Monitoring the quality of field experiences through ongoing communication between students and faculty supervisors; and
5. Engaging in debriefing seminars upon return.[21]

While Drolet identifies these components as mainly critical for the planning of longer-term international practicums, I maintain that they are important for any IEL program, whether it be a short, reading-break-type program or a longer-term, immersive practicum-type experience. In either case, collaborative networked teaching and learning is an ideal tool for facilitating these goals over the long term.

---

17. Ibid.
18. Ibid., 4.
19. Ibid.
20. Ibid.
21. Julie Drolet, "Getting Prepared for International Experiential Learning: An Ethical Imperative," in *Globetrotting or Global Citizenship*, 191ff.

Building and Sustaining International Field Partnerships and Relationships

The importance of building equitable and collaborative relationships across cultural differences was discussed in chapter 2. Drawing on Jacques Derrida's reflections on hospitality with Michael Bakhtin's theory of the ever-provisional characteristic of language, Loewen posits that "hospitality" characterizes the attitude required for teaching via collaborative online teaching because the efforts involved in planning a collaborative session require teachers to be "open" not only to each other, but to whatever surprises arise from that collaboration. The processes of creating a session plan for learning involve real-time communication, which not only demands vulnerability, reciprocity, and mutuality of interactions, but also requires an openness to surprises or what often are misrecognized as "failures" or "mistakes." The mutual respect offered each other in these instances is part of the recognition that all the participants are simultaneously foreigners and at home vis-à-vis each other's virtual presence. This is the kind of trust enacted by teachers and learners in the networked collaborative class sessions.

Marrying this concept of hospitality to Bakhtin's concept of dialogical expression reorients the relation between the "guest participant" and the "host institution/ community" to one of co-hosting, a mutually hospitable dialogical exchange. Since most, if not all, IEL programs involve a northern participant traveling to impoverished southern countries, this reorientation opens IEL programs to the potential of receiving participants from the global South to experience the social injustice and poverty of northern Canadian reserves, or American inner-city poverty and violence. Using collaborative networked teaching and learning in the context of preparing for an IEL program has the potential to raise big questions of social location, the contingency of birth, the postcolonial legacy of colonization, and the like before participants leave their home countries. While the immersive element of IEL is difficult to replicate virtually, using available technologies to prepare participants has the potential to enhance the in-country experience while facilitating the active and equal involvement of the co-hosting institution and local community, thus building reciprocal hospitality into all aspects of the IEL experience. This effort, using the techniques Loewen presents, has the potential to build and sustain international field partnerships and relationships that are more equitable then the monodialogical North/South relationship that often characterizes IEL partnerships.

Developing Mutually Agreed-Upon Learning Arrangements

Much of chapters 3 and 4 is devoted to this component of IEL preparation. While the nature of the IEL experience (i.e., long term, short term, work study, practicum, etc.) will influence the development of mutually agreed-upon learning goals and objectives, the iterative design process of collaborative course through the "times-three" guideline outlined in chapter 3 is an important tool for developing these learning arrangements. This iterative design process closely corresponds with the hermeneutic pedagogy I discussed in my response to chapter 2, and Kolb's experiential model of:

Experience → Observation/Reflection → Understanding → Testing/Evaluation of New Concepts → Repeat

Collaborative networked teaching and learning adds to this process by introducing a methodology for developing a consistent synchronous planning processes that does not necessarily require face-to-face, transnational meetings. Where in the past IEL coordinators/instructors would be required to make frequent international trips to develop these learning arrangements and to build and sustain international field partnerships and relationships, collaborative networked teaching and learning opens the process to virtual synchronous meetings.

Language Acquisition/Cultural Preparation and Debriefing

I am treating these two considerations under the same heading, as they are closely related. The virtual synchronicity of collaborative networked teaching and learning is well suited to support language acquisition and cultural preparation before departure and to provide both a continuing opportunity for building community and a means to engage both co-housing communities in debriefing and integration seminars. While language acquisition for short-term IEL programs is unlikely, predeparture cultural sensitivity and literacy is almost a universal aspect of successful IEL programs. By adding a collaborative networked learning experience to these predeparture programs, participants can be introduced to the culture they will

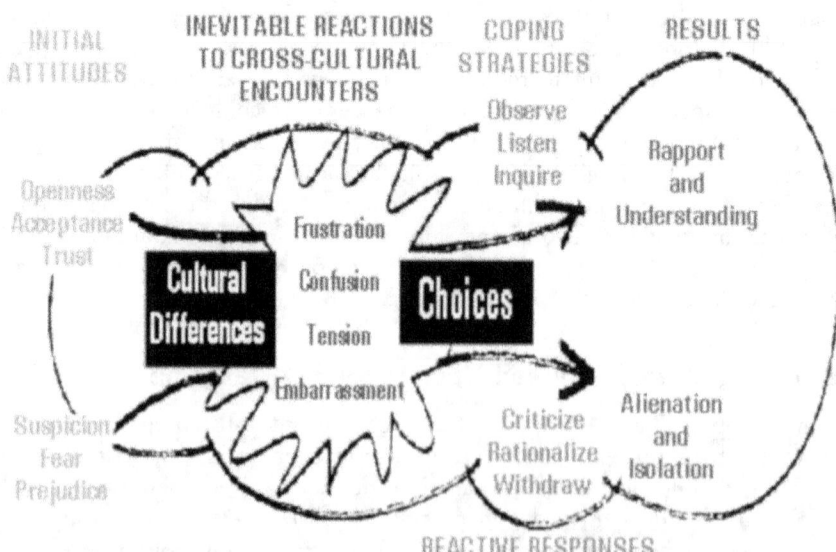

Taken from *Cross-Cultural Connections* by Duane Elmer, copyright © 2002 Duane H. Elmer. Used by permission of InterVarsity Press (www.ivpress.com).

experience, in real time, by those who will be co-hosting them. Actively involving those who will receive the IEL participants by participating in the pre- and postdeparture program lessens the "othering" effect that is often the unintended consequence of these programs. As with Derrida's concern over the "othering" of difference, these predeparture programs often other the communities to which participants are sent. For instances, it is a common practice to warn participants of the potential for "culture shock." As the following image illustrates, culture shock presents cross-cultural encounters as inevitably leading to "frustration, confusion, tension, and embarrassment."

The result of this approach is, as Loewen notes in chapter 2, to balkanize and fetishize "'the Other' as somehow strange, unfamiliar, or improper." My own experience with so-called culture shock has actually been experienced in the reverse. For instance, when I was fifteen years old, I participated in a four-week immersive experience in East End Kingston, Jamaica. Not knowing what to expect, my experience of Jamaican culture was not as shocking as the above image would suggest. It was only when I returned to my suburban North American home that I noticed my mother had, in my absence, started using linen napkins. I was shocked with what seemed to me to be an unnecessary and expensive affectation of wealth. How could we use linen napkins when so mouths have no food to eat, let alone wipe away? While this is perhaps an extreme, somewhat immature fifteen-year-old's reaction, it illustrates how the principle of hospitality and dialogical exchange through synchronous technology has the potential to defetishize the othering of IEL through the mutuality of dialogical exchange. Including the co-hosting community in the postexperience reflection and integration further contributes to the building of sustainable and equitable international partnerships.

Monitoring the Quality of Field Experiences

While anecdotal evidence would suggest that field supervision is increasingly relying on synchronous technologies like Skype, for the most part these technologies are being used to offset the expense of international telephone rates with little attention being paid to the pedagogical benefits. Ongoing communication is a concern for long-term (six months or longer) IEL programs, including long-term internships and year-abroad programs, such as the Trent-Ecuador/Ghana programs. These programs involve students spending an entire academic year in Ecuador or Ghana and include traditional classes and service learning with local NGOs.

One of the challenges of these programs is that a significant portion of my school's cohort is overseas during their third year. When they return, the class ahead of them has graduated and the class behind them is either overseas themselves or unknown to them because they were overseas. This can create a situation where the returning group is isolated and in some cases alienated from their fellow students. This is an ideal situation for knocking a hole between classrooms. For instance, the overseas student's home institution and the co-hosting institutions in either Ecuador or Ghana could participate in a number of collaborative networked sessions that bring together Trent students, students from the co-hosting institution, and second-year students preparing for their own year-abroad program in the following year. Planning collaborative network predeparture/in-country/postexperience programs would overcome in part some of the challenges associated with reintegrating returning students into the university community, as well as provide an opportunity for continued dialogical exchange.

Chapter 5

The Plan

Nathan Loewen

At a Glance

This chapter will introduce a method for planning the specific structure of each collaborative learning session.

- Brief narrative of a collaborative networked learning session
- Incorporating technologies for a collaborative networked pedagogy
- Evaluating technologies for collaborative teaching and learning
- Introducing the session-planning template
- Effective collaborative engagement during networked sessions

What Does a Collaborative Networked Learning Session "Look" Like?

At 09h30 EDT (UTC: - 4 hours), TeacherZ leaves her office for her classroom; but along the way, she stops in at her building's IT center to pick up the mobile video-conferencing cart. Seeing someone familiar in the halls, she asks for help to guide the device into her classroom. By the time she arrives, there are people already filtering into the room, which itself has round tables that seat roughly ten people,

---

*QR code URL: http://www.profweb.ca/en/publications/real-life-stories/three-lessons-learned-from-virtual-team-teaching

and on each table are three desktop computers. After plugging in the videoconferencing unit and pressing the power button, she connects the cables in the manner shown to her during the presession testing demo where her institution's IT person was present. While the videoconferencing unit powers up, she moves over to the teacher podium in order to turn on the room's computer and LCD projector.

TeacherZ continues to casually welcome people entering the room while writing the session's learning goals, a set of basic instructions, and a list of activities on the whiteboard. By this time, 09h45, the room is full with people pulling up chairs, chatting with colleagues, and setting out their writing pads. A few have laptops, and most of them have smartphones that they periodically check.

TeacherZ has a smartphone, too, and she sends a text message to TeacherA, telling him that she will be ready to connect at 10h00. TeacherA texts back to say, "Great! I will call to connect our VCU to yours." Using smartphone messages is the backchannel that these collaborators have agreed upon for communication outside the view of their learners. In the next five minutes, TeacherZ logs into Google Drive and opens the documents that will be used for the class session.

At 10h00 a call comes in on the videoconferencing unit. TeacherZ answers, and the other class appears. Both groups of students are not paying attention to the screen; the teachers have agreed to have their videoconference connection muted until they are ready to begin the actual session. By doing this, they are mitigating the potential for a cacophony of people getting settled into class.

TeacherZ calls for everyone's attention, and she confirms that today's class will be a collaborative networked learning session. She refers to the fact that they can see TeacherA doing something likewise on the videoconference screen. TeacherZ asks everyone to power up the desktop computers at their tables, and then she briefly confirms the basic guidelines for collaborative networked sessions. Near the beginning of the term, these guidelines were co-created by the two classes themselves as a sort of "collaborative networked learning contract." That was their first experience working in real time to create an online document, but by now they are very familiar with that kind of activity.

Someone mentions that it looks like the other class is ready. TeacherZ confirms this with a text message to TeacherA, who gives a "thumbs up" through the videoconference connection. It is now 10h10, but these extra minutes to ensure preparation help everyone feel as though the session will not be rushed, especially the teachers! Both teachers unmute their videoconferencing units, and begin a short discussion of the session's learning goals, basic instructions, and activities.

During Skype conversations to prepare for the session, the teachers agreed upon these and assembled everything needed for the session with online documents. These were circulated to the class earlier, along with the short video and text that the teachers expected their classes to review. Both teachers could see on their shared online platform that the learners had indeed posted short personal responses to the video and text. Many had posted their responses at the last minute using their smartphones. This was to be expected; but in any case, a basic activation to the session topic was already in place.

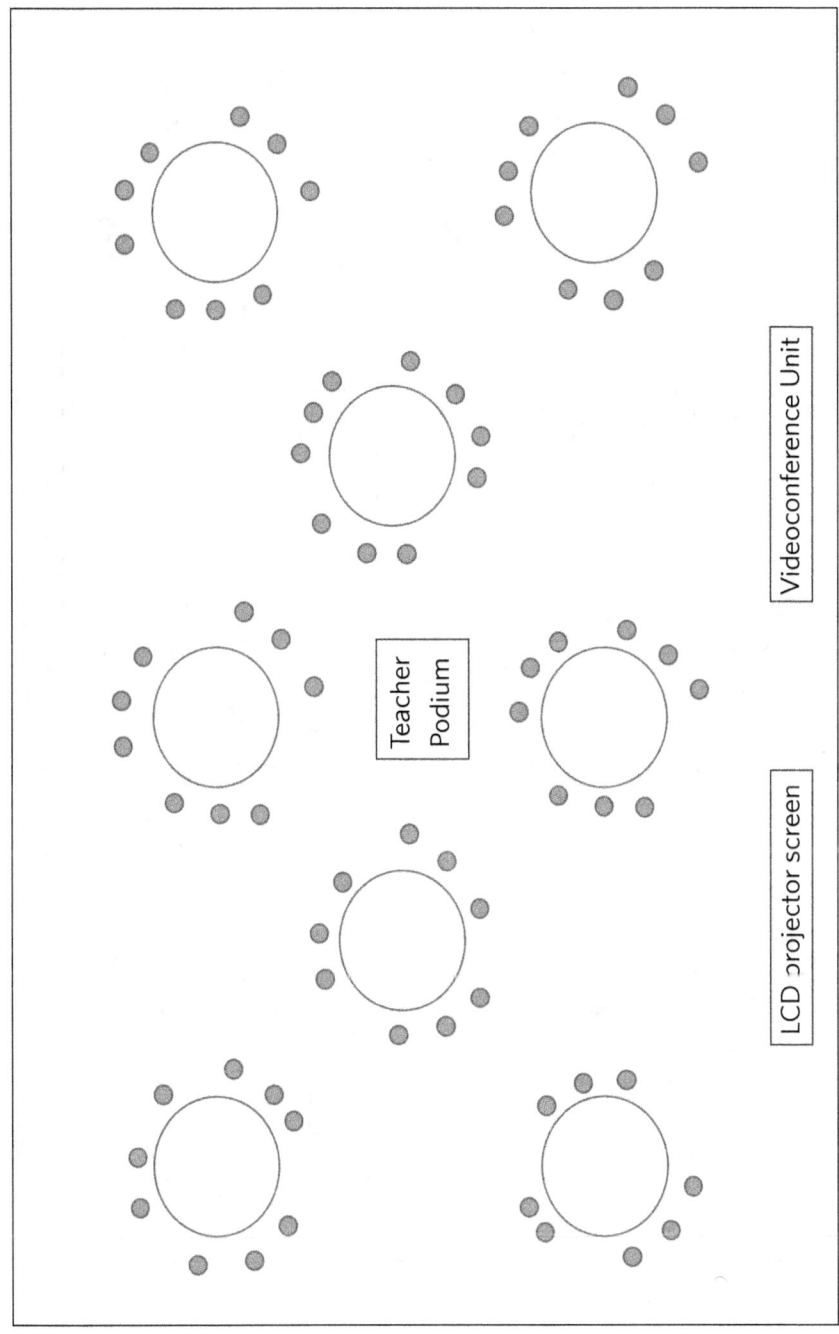

Teacher Z's Classroom Set-up

Teacher A's Classroom Set-up

After the session overview, TeacherA takes over to initiate the first activity. Considerable thought was put into the positioning of the videoconference unit at an earlier point in time. Each teacher positioned the unit's camera so that they could address both sets of students without putting their backs to either group. They had also obtained a long extension-corded microphone that they placed in the center of their rooms. While the microphone transmits almost all classroom sounds, this also means that both groups can casually discuss a topic together and hear each other perfectly. At one point in the term, everyone laughed when a "phantom sound" was emitted. No one in either room took responsibility!

The first activity is a version of "think-pair-share." It is based on the responses that were posted, where groups from each class are to review and summarize the responses of their classmates across the videoconference connection. This activity is accompanied by an instruction sheet that guides the learners in how to process the responses and what, specifically, the teachers are asking them to be sure to remark upon. After roughly five minutes, each group comes up to the videoconference unit and stands in a manner similar to their teachers. A series of brief conversations ensue, where groups confirm or add to what others have ascertained. The topical activation is accomplished. Everyone understands what they are discussing and the framework that the teachers are asking them to use for processing the topic.

The time is now 10h45, and there is only another twenty-five minutes remaining in the class session. TeacherA texts TeacherZ to ask about initiating the next activity. There is not a lot of time remaining in the class session, since there was more time used than expected by the introduction, explanation, and activation activity. The teachers agreed in advance, however, not to rush through the session plan. This can only lead to the kinds of misunderstandings and frustrations that lead to the breakdown of communication and collaboration. In the planning phase, the teachers did discuss how the main activity could be initiated in one collaborative networked session, and then completed in a future class session. Given the situation, TeacherZ texts to say that she will initiate the next activity and also to inform the classes that the activity would be completed in the next class session.

TeacherZ asks for everyone's attention, and then directs the classes to an online location with folders for each set of groups. Inside their folder are document, spreadsheet, and video files. As a larger group spanning both locations, each folder's contents outlines a case study and problem to be addressed. The learners are asked to follow the guide to create a solution to the problem collaboratively. The explanation of their solution is to be presented graphically, using an online presentation platform.

Each small group is made up of learners from the different geographical locations. In order to facilitate their communications with each other without creating cacophony in actual classrooms, the learners use the "chat" function built into the Google Docs interface. The chat facilitates the spontaneous, real-time conversations within each group. The "insert comment" function is used when a learner wishes to suggest a substantive piece of text or to identify a revision. In this manner, the screens show a fast-scrolling chat as learners communicate back and forth.

The room is filled with the chatter of keyboards. Slowly but surely, the documents begin to fill in with text, images, tables, and graphs.

> ### Extend the Innovation 5.1
>
> G. Brooke Lester
>
> There's nothing quite like watching a Google Doc take shape, at multiple hands, in real time, like a self-organizing work of art, don't you find?
> In 2012, as part of Digital Writing Month (or #DigiWriMo), aspiring digital artists descended onto Twitter and Google Docs, collaborating to write a poem in thirty minutes.[1] Emboldened by their success, organizers Jesse Stommel and Sean Morris facilitated a similar poetry-writing event in 2014, this time with the added twist that participants were free to change the rules midevent.[2] Oh, and there were a couple of novels, one about a duck.[3]
> This is all to say, go ahead and go nuts. A Google Doc allows as many as fifty contributors to collaborate simultaneously in a single document. As Loewen notes, "back channels" abound to facilitate the action: Google Docs' own built-in chat client, text messaging, Twitter, and so forth. You've got your networked classrooms together, so honor that synchronous moment by letting the learners get raucous together and learn by building.

After setting the videoconference units to "mute," the cross-class groups set to work, and TeacherA and TeacherZ circulate virtually through the online presentation platform and its chatting function. The teachers are thereby able to assess each group's progress; by texting each other, they are able to plan out coordinated interventions with each group. Affirmations, reminders, and suggestions are given to the groups by the collaborating teachers, sometimes singly and sometimes in tandem.

With only ten minutes remaining in the class session, TeacherA asks TeacherZ to begin the wrap-up of the collaborative networked session. They unmute their videoconferencing units and ask the groups to pause their work and ensure that they save their materials. TeacherA remarks that groups may continue to work on the cases outside of class, but that twenty minutes would be reserved for completing the analysis during the next session. TeacherA then asks the classes to do a CAT (classroom assessment technique): they should go to where their personal responses were posted, and then make a new post to summarize briefly one of the

---

1. You can see the results taking shape—with yodeling—on the front page of the DigiWriMo site (http://www.digitalwritingmonth.com/), or at YouTube (http://youtu.be/qT8GrKy130A).
2. Jesse Stommel and Sean Michael Morris, "Done Hooray! Collaborative Digital Poem," http://bit.ly/digpoem. Stommel and Morris are leading editors of Hybrid Pedagogy, of which Stommel is a co-creator, http://www.hybridpedagogy.com/about-us/.
3. These are *Digi Daze* (http://www.digitalwritingmonth.com/2012/11/01/a-novel-in-a-day/), and *Last Words: Goodnight, My Kitten* (http://makertext.com).

following: How has my position changed? What have I learned? What do I need to know? Or, what is not making sense to me?

At this point, the teachers say goodbye to each other and close the videoconference connection. The learners finish the CAT using their smartphones, laptops, and table computers, and TeacherZ begins shutting down the videoconference unit, classroom computer, and LCD projector. As they filter out of the room, TeacherZ has time to do the "usual" conversations and exchanges about upcoming assignments and ideas about the collaborative networked class session. One particularly interested person helps TeacherZ cart the videoconference unit back to the building's IT center.

TeacherZ then returns to her office, and opens a debriefing document in order to reflect on the session. She completes her reflections on the class session, and then gathers her materials to head off to another class. Later that week, she has scheduled a time to meet with TeacherA. Both of them individually completed a debriefing reflection, and they will compare notes in order to prepare for the next collaborative networked session. They might find a reason to go back to their original session plans and make some modifications, particularly since the case-study activity is now a part of the next class session.

TeacherZ and TeacherA's Collaborative Networked Session

The narrative above approximates an actual collaborative networked teaching and learning session. Throughout the account, you can observe two teachers using various technologies and platforms in order to bring together their classes. The technology is a means to an end: facilitating contact between the two classrooms and enabling the sharing of perspectives in real time across geographical distances.

Importantly, the account shows how the teachers worked to prepare themselves and the learners in such a way as to have structured flexibility during the actual session. The tacit emphasis on a reasonable pace, facilitated through a backchannel for communication between the teachers, enables the learning experience to avoid seeming rushed. Patience is a virtue where the emphasis of the activities is on communication among the learners; anything that causes communication breakdown is to be avoided. Gaps in understanding are something completely different from communication breakdown. Because the learners have time to identify and work with gaps amongst themselves, they can actually participate in the social construction of their knowledge about the topic and its complexities.

Hopefully, this vignette provides a sense of how plans unfurl into actuality with a collaborative networked teaching and learning session.

Technologies and Collaborative Networked Teaching and Learning

A question has been allowed to linger throughout this book and up until this chapter. Namely, What is the role of technology in the teaching and learning experience? The rationale for delaying the question was that the emphasis should always be set upon pedagogy, where technology is in service of the objectives and goals established by the collaborating teachers. The approach of this book is to see technology and teaching as discretely separated from each other, and the former is in service of the latter. In this chapter, where the actual plan for the collaborative networked session is discussed, the question concerning technology is allowed to arise.

The previous chapters encourage an iterative planning process, where collaborating teachers cycle through movements of unstructured sharing, creation of learning objectives, movement toward learning goals, and discussion of activities that support teaching and learning. After teachers know what they wish to accomplish and what they wish to do, then it is possible to move through another iteration of the planning process to add the detail of technologies.

Choosing Technologies

Choosing the most adequate technological tools for the learning goals is something partly determined by the activities themselves. The discussion of the activities, however, might be influenced in the iterative process by considering what technological possibilities are available for use in the collaboration. There are different applications for communication tools across the course of preparation for the actual in-class session. Communications technologies are already in use by the teachers who work through the planning process, and this extends to how the technologies that facilitate teaching are different from those used for learning.

For learning, the following principles for choosing technology may limit decisions depending upon the shared socioeconomic context of the classes at both institutions. The collaborating teachers must keep in mind that there cannot be a "digital divide" between their classes. There cannot be the presumption that one class will have ease of access to a technology or platform that the other class does not. Therefore, the basic requirements for selecting a technology must be considered with a clear and common understanding of the context for both classes:

- *Widely available*: There needs to be a high diffusion of the technology in question. Otherwise, there will be unequal accessibility. Availability takes a different form, case by case. For example, perhaps there is a one-in-three diffusion of personal laptops, but the campus IT department loans out laptops. Or, one class may all have personal smartphones, but the other class has nearly none.

- *Legally available*: No one should be required to obtain platforms or licenses without respecting copyright. If not, one or more persons or institutions will be unequally liable for misconduct. Not everyone has Microsoft Office, but anyone can download and use OpenOffice, and Google Docs can be accessed by anyone with an email account. Moodle and Canvas provide open-source Learning Management Systems within which class-to-class interactions can be arranged, whereas Blackboard is an LMS that requires an institution to purchase a license.

- *Readily affordable (either to the learners or their institution)*: Affordability is related to diffusion. Institutions or persons should not be expected to spend more than they otherwise would to participate, particularly if the collaboration is experimental or single-use.
- *Easily implemented, or training may easily be provided*: This is a case-by-case issue. One teacher's "easy" may be another's "impossible," and these variations will also run among the people within a class. Frank and open discussions should precede any attempts at training. Even if all of the above basic requirements are met, there should not be an irresolvable inequality of implementation or training. The collaboration may very well be capacity building, but, as with the prior requirement above, the return on investment should not be limited to an experiment or single-use.
- *Clearly understood limits for application, or, a clear understanding of how the technology may be open to creative application* (i.e., "hacked"): Put otherwise: everyone involved should have no false beliefs and offer no overestimations concerning the potential for a technology's utility. For example, most people use Prezi as a presentation platform. Upon discovering the "multiuser" aspect of Prezi, however, one teacher immediately adapted it to create a fun classroom assessment tool where learners "zoomed" from one question to the next and input their various answers.
- *Quickly communicates an application for learning*: As with the prior requirement, any technology should not deliver its pedagogical outcome via byzantine twists, turns, and promises. One sentence should be able to describe its application to teaching and learning; this will enable learners to understand clearly why they are using the application.
- *Respects bandwidth equity*: Along with diffusion and affordability, technology can become frustratingly useless if there is a bandwidth "bottleneck" or lack of infrastructural support. A rocket motor is useless when strapped to an oxcart, and an oxcart should not be expected to carry Mount Kilimanjaro. In other words, a videoconferencing unit cannot use low bandwidth, and a tablet running Skype lacks the ability to represent the input of an entire group of people.

The overall point being made by the basic requirements was already discussed in chapter 2: a strong and productive collaboration will actively work to address power differentials. Technology plays a role in creating power differences whenever there are disproportions of possession or access to information. These basic requirements must be met by everyone in both classes, otherwise there will be an insurmountable digital divide whose inequalities will create substantial dead ends for collaborative learning. These may be met either by the individual learners or, as in most cases, by the institution. You may find your options narrowing as a result.

Extend the Innovation 5.2

Christopher J. Duncanson-Hales

Perhaps with the exception of chapter 1, a theme that has been threading its way through my responses has been the place of power differentials in collaborative networked teaching and learning. In this chapter, Loewen reiterates the critical importance of addressing these power differentials as a basic requirement for successful and productive collaborations. "Technology," he notes, "plays a role in creating power differences whenever there are disproportional possession or access to technology and information. The basic requirement of digital access must be met by everyone in both classes, otherwise there will be an insurmountable digital divide whose inequalities will create substantial dead-ends for collaborative learning." As he emphasizes, the challenge of this *digital divide* cannot be overstated or ignored, and for that reason I would like to spend some time unpacking this concept.

In the session narrative above, TeacherZ and TeacherA had institutional access to high-level technology options. This is not always the case. Their learning activities could just as easily have taken place with vastly different technological options. The teachers might have made a speakerphone call with their smartphones. Or, they might have used Skype, which requires only a 256k bandwidth connection for voice-only communications. If they used a simple, open LMS like Moodle, the teachers might have organized their classes to communicate using wikis and forums. This would have required several days' coordination rather than one real-time session. A real-time communication exchange could take place if enough people had smartphones, and the teachers could have organized a series of text-message exchanges among groups of phone numbers. The main point is to think about what various technologies and modes of communication can enable the kind of activity that is envisioned to realize the learning goals.

What Kinds of Technologies Are Out There?

As noted in the paragraph above, the options available to collaborating teachers are open to adjustment and experimentation. Previous collaborative networked learning sessions have been facilitated strictly by email, and sometimes by telephone. These cases typically involve a collaborations with remote or rural institutions, or institutions in developing countries. The value of collaborative learning is likely higher in these scenarios, too, since the teachers and learners are far more aware of the need and importance of bridging differences to enable communication. There are several ways of breaking down the distinctions among the information and communication technologies that may be available.

Virtual Meeting Tools

Virtual meeting tools function over the Internet, either from IP address to IP address or via a Web-based platform, to allow for multiple parties to view and hear each other. Depending upon the degree of bandwidth available to each party involved, these tools may provide only voice connections. There are other external factors that impinge upon the quality of the connection that have been experienced by collaborative networked teaching and learning projects in the past: the Olympics, for example, were streamed over the Internet. During the time of major events, as a result, the quality of connections were severely degraded to the point of being dysfunctional. The same sort of phenomenon can happen over a smaller scale when institutions or their regions experience "peak Internet." Generally speaking, there is greater bandwidth available in early mornings than in the afternoons. The main point is that if even one of the participating connections is hampered by these external factors, then the quality of the entire collaborative session is likely to be compromised. As will be noted in chapter 6, testing technology *must* take place during the time of intended use in order to simulate whether or not bandwidth problems may be an issue.

Virtual meeting tools that rely on videoconferencing are the only kinds of devices specifically made for group-to-group video interactions. Most use wide-angle cameras and multidirectional microphones. These devices typically provide the highest-quality connections. This applies globally as well as locally, where collaborative networked learning sessions have very successfully taken place between Montreal, New Delhi, and Moscow. There are many complexities involved in the operation of videoconferencing units that have to do with how such units communicate with each other. The major brands (Sony, Tandberg, Polycom, and LifeSize) previously excluded each other using proprietary technologies, but device-agnostic videoconferencing protocols are slowly becoming standardized.

The variety of ways that teachers and learners may communicate in real time is constantly changing. A definitive list of means for simultaneous communication may not be possible, but all of the following are successfully used by teachers and learners for collaborative networked teaching and learning. The following list will likely be outdated before this book is printed, or the names and relevant Web links to these items may change due to the vicissitudes of business, marketing, and other functions of capitalism:

- Cellular phones: Texting and voice options are available, and these work well for collaborations within the same country. Of particular value is their use by teachers for a communications backchannel.

- There are several online platforms that use "WebRTC" and "HTML5" to enable video conversations within browsers such as Chrome, Opera, and Firefox. These may or may not work within Explorer and Safari.

  – Appear.in—One-click video conversations with up to eight people.

  – vLine—Very easy conversations, "copy, paste, video chat."

  – Another easy video conversation tool.

- There are many "Voice Over Internet Protocol" (VoIP) apps. Anyone who plays Massively Multiplayer Online Games will know several VoIP platforms, such as Ventrilo and Mumble.

- Google offers a variety of platforms that work within their Google Apps environment. You are most likely familiar with Gmail, which can support Google Voice to enable calls to phones from your Gmail, or Google Hangouts, which also use "WebRTC."

- Skype is possibly the best-known communications application, partly because its purchase by Microsoft has led to wider distribution throughout the world and higher-quality service.

- Not to be left out of the real-time communications game, Facebook also supports video calling.

- For the possibility of international calling and messaging, several collaborative projects have reported the usefulness of a platform called Viber.

- There is the option of Apple's FaceTime application, but it only works if everyone has an Apple device. The affordability and diffusion of Apple products may be insufficient to make this a reliable option.

The platforms and applications mentioned above are "free," for the most part. They may require investments in other technology, such as computers, Web cameras, screens, and microphones. All of them are severely limited in that they are created for *individual* face-to-face communication, rather than group-to-group communication. As a result, consideration must be given to their implementation. Additionally, there are many more "paywalled" communications options, such as Adobe Connect, but these options require substantially more investment than most teachers, individuals, and institutions would be willing to make.[4]

Virtual Collaboration Tools

Collaborative networked teaching and learning relies not only on video and audio connections, but just as much on a wide variety of whatever tools are available that enable teachers and learners to communicate with each other in real time or serially. Just as with any other aspect of online applications and commerce, the scope of potential tools available to be used for collaborative teaching and learning is rapidly changing. Companies merge or fail. Companies rebrand, "update," or overhaul platforms and their functions. New innovations or longstanding platforms may appear or disappear at will. All of this is to say that the range of available platforms and tools is subject to being ephemeral. The following is a generic list of possible tools, therefore, without providing Web links to their current providers:

---

4. QR code URLs: (1) https://appear.in/; (2) https://vline.com/; (3) http://www.sightline.com/; (4) http://www.ventrilo.com/; (5) http://wiki.mumble.info/wiki/Main_Page; (6) http://www.google.com/intl/en/chat/voice/; (7) https://www.google.com/+/learnmore/hangouts/; (8) http://www.skype.com/en/; (9) https://www.facebook.com/videocalling/; (10) http://www.viber.com/; (11) https://www.apple.com/mac/facetime/; (12) http://www.adobe.com/products/adobeconnect.html.

- Document-sharing platforms, such as Google Drive, OneDrive (formerly SkyDrive), Box, which is distinct from Dropbox, and so on.
- Online curation platforms, such as Pinterest, Scoop.it!, Knovio, 123Dcatch, Haiku Deck.
- Information curation applications such as OneNote on Microsoft 365, Evernote, Google Keep, Quip.
- Blogging platforms such as Blogger, WordPress.
- Microblogging applications such as Twitter, Tumblr, Google+, Twister.
- Collaborative presentation applications such as Prezi, Realtime board, TitanPad, Google Presentation, Vyew, Scriblink, Dabbleboard, Storybird, and Storify.
- A variety of "paywalled" collaboration platforms such as VIA from SvieSolutions, Adobe Connect, etc.
- A variety of "paywalled" Learning Management Systems with collaborative tools inside their licenses such as BlackBoard Collaborate, Instructure Canvas, Sakai from AsahiNet.
- Moodle is a free, open-source LMS that stands apart from the previous point primarily because it can be implemented for a far lesser cost than those systems. Within Moodle is the typical range of potentially collaborative tools such as blogs, wikis, and forums. And, if one is up to it, the Moodle community is often capable of coming up with a solution for a different collaborative issue free of charge. There is, however, the "sweat equity" of learning how to implement the solution!
- Adapting virtual project-management approaches from the business world can easily be used for online collaborations, with platforms such as Podio, Basecamp, and activeCollab.
- Social media can provide private groups within which exchanges may take place. Facebook is best known, but other platforms exist such as Google+, Yammer, or Edmodo.
- Literally any online platform or application might be adapted to collaborative teaching and learning. The basic requirements listed earlier in this chapter need only be applied for such considerations.

No matter what technologies are chosen to facilitate the learning goals of a collaborative networked session, the choice must be made with an eye toward the involvement and participation of all possible stakeholders. The meaning of this will be explored further in chapter 6. Suffice to say at this point, any decision made by collaborating teachers needs to include consultation with others in their institutions. They are "stakeholders" because their interests are affected by the activities of the collaboration. These stakeholders include the IT personnel and relevant administrators. Websites and applications such as Facebook, Google Drive, or YouTube may either be blocked or throttled by your institution's network, or your decision to use them might violate a policy with a name such as "Computer Resources Acceptable Use and Security Policy." Regular, friendly, and clear communications with IT staff and relevant administrators can save a collaborative project from being blocked due to poor consultation in the decision to use technologies and platforms.

The Session-Planning Template

A detailed plan should be constructed once decisions have been made about the selection of technologies and platforms to facilitate a collaborative networked session. In order to guide the collaborative planning process, this chapter includes a collaborative networked session template. The following template can be recreated quite simply with the use of a word-processing program, or, preferably, an online document-sharing platform such as Google Documents.

Using a session-planning template enables each partner teacher to understand clearly what will happen in a given collaborative session. It is a common location where teachers can place the results of their iterative planning process, as well as set forth the relevant details for the enactment of the actual collaborative session. The planning for the session can never be too "granular," which is to say that there is a corresponding level of learner success and teacher effectiveness with the higher degrees of detail in a shared planning document. Creating a "record" of a collaboration through something such as an email thread has, in nearly all experiences, lead to disastrous blunders or abandonment prior to the actual session. A session-planning template provides a shared location where everyone involved in the planning process can articulate their shared vision, expectations, and accountability.

In terms of planning, there is an insufficient level of detail given in the narrative of the example collaborative networked learning session at the beginning of this chapter. Session plans should be clear and yet deal with the minutiae of what the teachers set out to accomplish. Where and whenever possible, collaborating teachers should always have a "Plan B"-type of scenario available for every part of their session. If not, they should at least have discussed how any planned element, during the actual realization of the session, may be modified, improvised, deferred, delayed, or deleted. This is the reason for the importance of having a backchannel for teacher-to-teacher communications. As noted in the example narrative, this backchannel did allow for TeacherZ and TeacherA to make a decision about extending their primary activity into the next class session. This luxury may not always be available, however, and collaborating teachers should therefore clearly and deliberately rank the importance of each planned element. What can go? What *must* stay? What is optional?

Collaborative Networked Teaching Session Template			
Session Number and/or Title: Date of In-Class Session: Time of In-Class Session (UTC): Lesson Topic:			
	Pre-session Preparation	**Responsible**	**Done?**
Learning Outcomes: (Use Bloom's Taxonomy?)	• To generate . . . • To assemble • To reflect . . . •		
Technical Preparation:	• Reserve laptops . . . •		
Online Materials Preparation	• Upload worksheets onto Google Drive . . . • Preparatory reading and forum questions . . . •		
	Minute-by-minute scenario of in-session activities:		
Pre-Connection: Duration:	• Set up . . . • Organize students into groups • Students log into their Google docs •		
Introductions: Duration:	• Teachers introduce each other • Teachers introduce the topic • Students say hello through connection • Introduce focus of the class •		
1st Activity: Duration:	• Have students use the worksheet in order to . . . •		
2nd Activity: Duration:	• introduce concept . . . •		
Additional Activities	Insert rows below		
Closing/Summary Duration:	• Review events of the session . . . • Classroom assessment technique: GoogleForm survey • Concludiing observations . . . •		
	Post-session activities		
Immediately After Class:	Return laptops . . . Upload results onto Google Drive . . .		
Teacher Follow-up:	• Collate and post survey results on Moodle . . . • Complete debriefing template • Meet online for debriefing discussion •		
Student Follow-up:	• Meet with group members on Skype • Complete wiki on Moodle •		

This is only an example of what has worked in the past. Feel free to reproduce and adapt this template to your specific needs.

Extend the Innovation 5.3

G. Brooke Lester

"Huh. It looks as if the projector isn't going to work. Oh, and your handouts jammed the copy machine. Sorry."

When you're prepared to hear these words, and to suffer only a momentary onset of fight-or-flight before calmly taking the podium, then (and only then) are you ready for your presentation. I mutter them to myself while driving Sunday mornings to churches that have invited me to lead adult-education series. And I teach them to my students while they prepare to do professional-quality in-class presentations in my advanced-level seminars.

What makes it possible? It's more than knowing your "material"; it's knowing your *narrative*. Every (decent) presentation has one. If you know the story you're trying to tell, and care enough about it to present it positively and *want* it to be heard, then you're ready to go . . . with or without the kindness of the Fates.

What's true for a solo presentation is true for a networked class session. The session isn't in the "deck," or slides; it isn't in the planned activities; it isn't even in the networked connection. The session is in the narrative. Know the narrative, and "Plan B" (and Plans C, D, and E) will reveal themselves.

Merlin Mann and Dan Benjamin have a good conversation on "the narrative" and presentations in their podcast "Sorry. You Can't Have a Candle." Start at the seventeen-minute mark if you want to skip the social preliminaries.[5]

The progression of activities should be planned to the minute. Where possible, the planned durations ought to be adhered to, but as noted in the session narrative, it is so much better that sessions "flow" and not be rushed than for their activities to take place precisely within the planned times. That said, teachers should realistically plan for how much time any given activity may occupy. For example, there should definitely and always be an allocation of sufficient time for adequate greetings, openings, closings, transitions, and goodbyes. These sorts of marker events are crucial for establishing a clear "flow" for the actual session.

Effective Collaborative Engagement During Networked Sessions

Leading an engaging collaborative networked learning session is largely a matter of adopting an all-encompassing scope and team-based practice of classroom management. People can quickly recognize when a set of partners is "out of sync" with each other, and those sorts of gaps in collaboration among the teachers quickly pass over to the learners in the forms of skepticism, disengagement, confusion, and frustration. For this reason, particularly high levels of self-consciousness and behavioral awareness need to be implemented by the collaborating teachers so that everyone is carried along in the learning experience.

---

5. QR code URL: http://5by5.tv/b2w/38.

- Establish and repeatedly reestablish a welcoming climate for participation.
  - Smile and speak slowly.
  - Be aware if anyone has a fear of the camera, microphone, or other technology.
  - Always make time for words of welcome and graceful closings.
  - Learn and use names of people in all locations.
  - Express interest in others.
  - Validate anyone's decision to participate.
  - Explain activity instructions and verify they are understood.
  - Repeat session learning goals.
  - Maintain an awareness of time and timing.
- Demonstrate awareness of all the geographically separated sites.
  - Speak to all participants as a whole, and never only to the other teacher.
  - Call on people from all locations.
  - Enable learners to engage each other across sites, and avoid the temptation to moderate, mediate, or translate between or among learners.
  - Speaking teachers should never have their backs to anyone at any location.
  - Ensure that the backchannel is open, activated, and checked regularly.
  - Explain all decisions to modify the session activities.
- Moderate all activities *across* the separated sites.
  - Give clear expectations of the learners.
  - Make learning goals explicit.
  - Provide concise explanations of upcoming activities.
  - Leave room for alternate questions or responses.
  - Allow for pauses in discussions.

Success Is in the Details

This chapter's aim was to provide the means for structuring the specifics of a collaborative networked teaching and learning session. The discussion of technology was finally introduced alongside a template for breaking down the fine details of the actual session. More details await, however! The next chapter moves through other considerations that will ensure the success of a collaborative project.

Chapter Response I—G. Brooke Lester
Assign "Fails" to Find Digital Learning Wins

In summer 2011, my school had a new "smart" classroom installed, including the capacity to live-stream presentations, invite interaction from viewers, and capture the results for later viewing.

Here in fall 2014, it has *almost* begun to work. (More accurately, *something* works pretty well . . . just not what we installed.)

So what happened?

The initial rig involved a podium with a touch-screen interface; presenters could connect their own laptop, or simply use the "Mac Mini" built in to the podium. A ceiling-mounted camera captured the podium area and whiteboard, and could be swiveled to most other areas of the room. Audience members needed only a Web browser to view the presentation synchronously (in real time), or the captured recording later. In either case, any given viewer would have two windows, one showing the presenter at the podium and the other showing her slideshow; the viewer, as he wished, could "toggle" these such that one window was enlarged and the other made smaller.

Then the conversations began.

> Me: "Say, let's find an event and test that rig, eh?"
>
> IT: "Well, it's not actually ready. Our builders left a lot of stuff undone. We're trying to get them back."
>
> Me: "Okay. I'll check back."

Later:

> Me: "So, it looks like they were back, connecting unconnected ethernet jacks and power plugs. Are we good on testing the presentation-capture?"
>
> IT: "Well, it's like this: our vendor went out of business. So, our subscription with them has disappeared. We're going to find another vendor."
>
> Me: ". . . Okay. I'll check back."

Later:

> Me: "Remember the presentation capture in the 'smart' classroom we built a year or two back?"
>
> IT: "Well, I'm going to have to go in there and see what's what. After all, we bought it a long time ago, and software falls out of date, and subscriptions retire. I'll see what the situation is."
>
> Me: ". . . Okay. Get back to me."

Obviously, something wasn't working. And this was an IT staff with which I have had (the evidence of this miniseries notwithstanding) a close, friendly, and usually productive relationship! Following some coincidental staff turnover, I tried the following.

> Me: "So, this fall, four months from now, I want to capture fifteen student presentations, while also live-streaming them. What's needed?"
>
> IT: "Well, the last guy said that nobody ever used that stuff, so he cannibalized it for other uses."
>
> Me: "So, this fall, in four months, I want to capture fifteen student presentations, while also live-streaming them. What's needed?"

This newer IT staff member took up the challenge, and began working through options with me. A repeated theme was, "We can use the remains of what's installed here, with these limitations and these unknowables. Or, we can work out another way that's much more likely to work well. Or, certain to work . . . maybe well." In *every* case, I said, "Let the past dead bury their own dead. Show me what you have in mind."

Today, at the midpoint of the semester, we've captured two student presentations per week for three weeks. A final piece of the previously installed set-up, probably in a show of spite, gave out on us in the second week. Now that that's past, we're ready to begin live-streaming in a modest way (promoting our student presentations via social media, anticipating that *literally tens of viewers* will gamely tune in to learn more about "The Old Testament in the New Testament" with us). The students will include their captured presentations in an online exhibit of their own making, introducing laypeople to our subject matter. With that end in view, they have professionalized their presentations beyond anything I have seen in previous seminars, which makes them more fun for everyone present. (And soon, for those not present!)

The IT staff and I are both jazzed that we have a "digital learning win" to bring to the administration, with a reality-based invitation for faculty or visitors to undertake similar or spin-off presentation projects.

Lessons learned:

- *Sunk costs are sunk costs*. It's tempting to say, "We've paid for this thing, and by gum, we're going to get something out of it." However, it may well be that if "this thing" is over three years old and unused, you'll spend less for better results if you abandon the past and look forward.

- *Low-stakes pilot projects*. Fifteen student presenters means fifteen "dress rehearsals" for the high-stakes, visiting-professor, audience-of-thousands event that you'll *really want to go well* a few months down the line.

- *Commit to a target*. "We're going to accomplish this event on this date. Start the countdown . . . now." Without a deadline, any new capabilities will live forever, cryogenically frozen, in the "Someday Maybe" file.

So, when Loewen says, "Regular, friendly and clear communications with IT staff and relevant administrators can save a collaborative project from being blocked due to poor consultation in the decision to use technologies and platforms . . . ," think on any anecdotes from your past that remind you of my own. Then, let the past dead bury their own dead, and think about how this might look in your future.

Chapter Response II—*Christopher J. Duncanson-Hales*
Minding the Divides

Mark Graham, in his article "Time Machines and Virtual Portals: The Spatialities of the Digital Divide," recognizes that the increased attention being paid to "overcoming" the digital divide is based on misguided temporal and spatial assumptions underpinning common accounts of the divide.

The "Digital Divide"

Oxford English Dictionary: **digital divide** *n.* (a) a division between those in favour of the extensive use of digital technology (esp. computers) and those against it; (b) (now the usual sense) the gulf between those who have ready access to current digital technology (esp. computers and the Internet) and those who do not; (also) social or educational inequality resulting from this.

- 1994 *U.S. Newswire* (Nexis) 9 Nov., AOL Chairman and CEO Steve Case said: 'There's no single solution to bridging the digital divide . . . We must take steps now so that in the Internet Century, no children are left behind.'
- 1995 *Columbus (Ohio) Disp.* 19 Dec. 8f, His take, though, is that the zealots on both sides of the digital divide are 'full of hooey'.
- 1996 G. A. Poole in *N.Y. Times* (Nexis) 29 Jan. d3/3 The digital divide between these two schools in the heart of Silicon Valley provides perhaps the most striking example anywhere in the nation of a widening gap.
- 2008 *Guardian* 7 Feb. (Technology section) 3/1 Initiatives such as the OLPC and the Classmate are intended to help bridge the digital divide. But security experts warn that there could be an unforeseen negative effect.[6]

The positive social and economic effects of the digital revolution, Graham reminds us, are not new but, rather, have their antecedents in similar arguments circulating during the development and expansion of the telegraph and telephones.

---

6. "digital divide, n." OED Online, September 2014, http://www.oed.com/view/Entry/52611?redirected From=digital+divide.

Graham recounts the opinion of Amos Dolbear, one of the inventors of the telephone who foresaw McLuhan's global village, arguing that "any device that enlarges one's environment and makes the rest of the world one's neighbors is an efficient mechanical missionary of civilization and help to save the world from insularity where barbarism hides."[7]

Underpinning this optimism, both then and now, is the twin ontological assumptions of a linear temporal/spatial conception of progress. Those who "have" are somehow ahead of and therefore better than those who "have not." The have-nots, to develop and progress, must catch up with the haves. Popular accounts of the digital divide assume a linear temporal concept of technological progress where terms like "catch-up" and "failing to keep up" with technological innovation temporally position societies in the global South as "backwards" and "behind." Graham notes that "irrespective of how any 'digital divide' discourse is formulated, the trope is always used to refer to a gap in capabilities and potentials and possibilities between different groups or places. Furthermore, a "digital divide" is never posited as a beneficial or positive outcome; it is, rather, something to be alleviated, filled, narrowed, reduced, stepped over, or shrunk." Graham concludes that "using ICT's (Information & Communication Technologies) to bridge a 'digital divide' is thus in many cases seen as a way of moving people along a pre-defined path of development."[8]

Spatially, the "digital divide" conceives not only a technical divide between access to technology, but also a physical divide between North/South, Urban/Rural, East/West, and so forth.[9] This physical divide is overcome by entering the *res cogitans* of cyberspace, which perceives the Internet as "a new kind of *non-physical space* [that] was almost guaranteed to attract 'spiritual' and even 'heavenly' dreams."[10] Cyberspace is thus conceptualized "as both an ethereal, alternate dimension which is simultaneously infinite and every (because everyone with an internet connection can enter), and as fixed in a distinct location, albeit a non-physical one (because despite being infinitely accessible, all willing participants are thought to arrive into the same marketspace, civic forum and social space). Cyberspace, in this sense, truly becomes a global village."[11]

Much like the shared virtual space portrayed in the movie *The Matrix*, cyberspace is a hybrid physical/virtual simulacrum. Symbolized in *The Matrix* by a telephone, with access to the right hardware, software, and ICT infrastructure, "all of the inhabitants of the earth would be brought into one intellectual neighborhood and be at the same time perfectly freed from those contaminations which might under other circumstances be received."[12]

---

7. Quoted in Mark Graham, "Time Machines and Virtual Portals: The Spatialities of the Digital Divide," *Progress in Development Studies* 11, no. 3 (July 1, 2011): 212.
8. Ibid., 215.
9. Ibid.
10. Margaret Wertheim, *The Pearly Gates of Cyberspace*, quoted in ibid., 216.
11. Ibid., 216.
12. Ibid.

The Hierarchy of Innovation

Following the postdevelopment critique of theorists like Ernesto Escobar, Mark Graham maintains that the uncritical acceptance of these assumptions, which has plagued much development theory and practice since Walter Rostow's stages of development, restricts our capacity to imagine alternatives beyond the Western, neoliberal, capitalist development paradigm of classical political economic theory. Or, as Escobar argues in the context of postdevelopment, there is a need to "to open up the discursive space to other ways of describing those conditions, less mediated by the premises and experiences of 'development.'"

These assumptions are being duplicated in some theorists' understanding of technological innovation, one can presume having a similar stunting effect. For instances, Nicholas Carr, former editor of the *Harvard Business Review*, in what he admits is a very rough idea, suggests that "If progress is shaped by human needs, then general shifts in needs would also bring shifts in the nature of technological innovation. The tools we invent would move through the hierarchy of needs, from tools that help safeguard our bodies on up to tools that allow us to modify our internal states, from tools of survival to tools of the self. Here's my crack at what the hierarchy of innovation looks like." The accompanying graphic presents

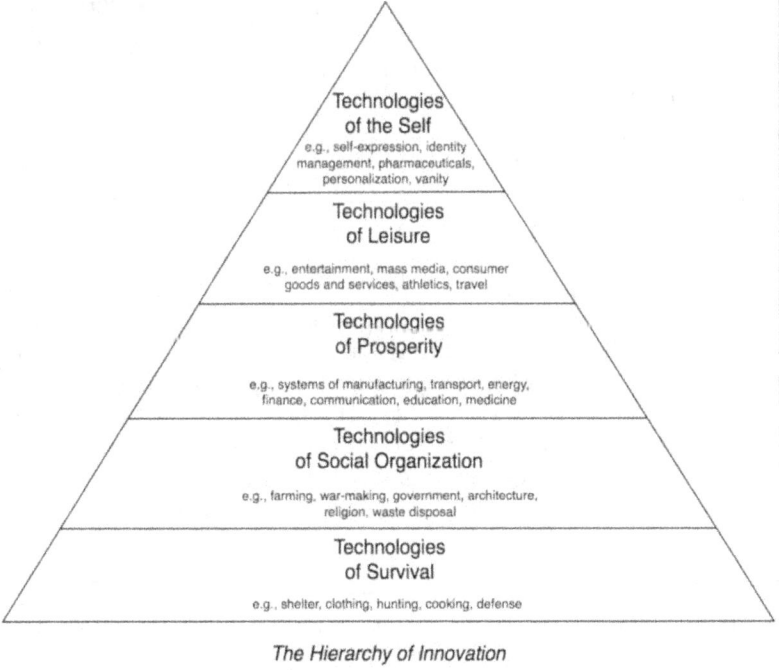

The Hierarchy of Innovation

Nicholas Carr's Hierarchy of Innovation. © Nicholas Carr (http://www.roughtype.com/?p=1603)

a hierarchal representation of technological progress where technologies of survival are at the base, and technologies of the self at the apex of the pyramid.[13]

With approximately two-thirds of the world's population living on less than two dollars a day,[14] one is tempted to invert Carr's hierarchy to privilege technologies of survival over technologies of the self.

It is these open spaces that are undermined by an ontological understanding of the "digital divide" as a global village, where "people and places can be separated into two groups: those with access to the 'global market place' and 'information revolution,' and those unable to gain access and participate."[15] Graham proposes an alternative formulation of the digital divide that avoids the excesses of the temporal linear understanding, "which take into account the hybrid, scattered, ordered and individualized nature of cyberspace."[16]

Cyberspace, Graham maintains, is "an evolution and extension of everyday spatial practice rather than a separate space." Quoting Julie Cohen, Graham argues that "cyberspace is in and of the real-space world, and is so not (only) because real-space sovereigns decree it, or (only) because real-space sovereigns can exert physical power over real-space users, but also and more fundamentally because cyberspace users are situated in real spaces."[17]

Loewen's analogy of holes between classrooms nicely captures this understanding of the "real-space" and "real-time" quality of cyberspace. With this image, he avoids the ontic nonspace of a third, otherworldly cyber-classroom that can be stepped into and shared by both classrooms. His classrooms exist in the real world as geographically separated real space in real-time classrooms. Collaborative networked teaching and learning is therefore not experienced in a "cyberspace" conceived "as an abstract Cartesian space, but instead [is] experienced [as a] spatiality mediated by embodied human cognition. Cyberspace in this sense is relative, mutable and constituted via the interactions among practice, conceptualization and representation."[18]

These connected classrooms are embedded in the sociocultural and political economic context and reality of their locality. Recognition of this real-time, real-space connection allows us to see beyond the digital divide as simply a lack of digital access that can be fixed with the right economic inputs. While, as Loewen notes, access to technology is a must for participation in collaborative networked teaching and learning, this is not only a problem of economics but of social, cultural, and political positionality. As Graham notes, a "myriad other factors related to the politics and practices of access (such as gender, class and age) can be as equally

---

13. Nicholas Carr, "The Hierarchy of Innovation," *Rough Type*, May 14, 2012, http://www.roughtype.com/?p=1603.
14. "Poverty Headcount Ratio at $2 a Day (PPP) (% of Population)," *World Bank IBRD-IDA*, http://data.worldbank.org/indicator/SI.POV.2DAY/countries/1W?display=map.
15. Graham, "Time Machines, 217.
16. Ibid., 211.
17. Julie Cohen,"Cyberspace and/as Space," quoted in ibid., 218.
18. Ibid., 220.

inhibitive as financial barriers."[19] A story Loewen told during a Skype meeting with Brooke Lester to discuss our responses to this text illustrates this point.

During one of our planning sessions, in response to a question about power differentials between classrooms, Loewen related how the basic requirement for technical access to the Internet was facilitated between a North American classroom and an African classroom. In this particular situation, the African classroom lacked a reliable Internet connection to facilitate a synchronous video session. To overcome this challenge, money was provided to the partnered instructor to rent out all the tables in a cybercafé so as to accommodate the technical requirements of the networked session. While the digital divide as presented here is easily resolved economically, there may have been other sociocultural conditions that required the exclusive use of the cybercafé.

For instance, Graham notes that "Telecentres and Internet cafes, for example, are often highly-gendered spaces and can be unwelcoming to women . . ."[20] For the sake of argument, assuming a co-ed class composition, in such an environment, the sociocultural barrier of gender may have required the instructor to secure exclusive use of the cybercafé so as to include his female students in the networked session. Thus, if an arrangement was not made to accommodate gender, then gender inequality can be seen as significant a challenge to participation as access to a reliable Internet connection.

Graham identifies other virtual divides that can be equally limiting. For instance, in North Korea, access to the Internet is limited to a handful of senior government officials. In France, access to Websites depicting Nazi memorabilia is restricted as are access in China and Saudi Arabia to sites considered a threat to their national security.[21]

What these examples illustrate is that, when planning for collaborative networked teaching and learning sessions, we need to be attentive not only to disproportional possession or access to hardware, software, and connection but also the sociocultural and political barriers that can restrict and or limit access to these tools. As was the case with the big questions raised by the rural/urban example in the previous example, attention to the sociocultural and political economic positionality of instructors and students will inevitably surface big ethical questions that, if anticipated, can be included in collaborative networked teaching and learning.

---

19. Ibid.
20. Ibid.
21. Ibid., 221.

Chapter 6

The Details

Nathan Loewen

At a Glance

Attending to important details will enable you and your partner to conduct a successful collaboration.

- Testing and simulation
- What to do: pre-, during, and postsession
- Effective debriefing for successful collaboration
- Fostering collaborative networks within institutions:
  - Administration: conveying value to decision makes
  - Advisory staff: sustaining collaborations
  - IT staff: collaborative etiquette

Getting Started on the Details

A new academic term is just underway as I write this, and "the details" are emerging as teachers conduct their initial collaborative networked sessions. All the preparations described in the earlier chapters of this book are complete. Since most

---

*QR Code URL: http://www.ascd.org/ASCD/pdf/journals/ed_lead/el_198602_bevoise.pdf

collaborations already began their planning over the summer, there are already set in place activities that are derived from clearly defined learning goals. The classes know these learning experiences will be a part of their term, and the class sessions are building toward these exciting events.

Now is the time when the details are to be looked after. And these details require a series of communications among different units and levels of the participating institutions. In particular, the collaborating teachers are testing the technologies involved in their activities. Sometimes this entails consultations with or the direct involvement of IT staff. Typically, as with teaching a new course or preparation, teachers and their institutions who are new to working collaboratively must invest themselves to determine just what the details are and how to manage the details correctly. Once there is more experience, these items become a part of the workflow and take very little time. This chapter will first focus on the important details of making sure that all the planned-for activities will work across the involved technologies and platforms. The chapter's discussion then moves to the next important detail: taking time for reflection and debriefing after a collaborative networked session. Finally, the chapter will consider the important detail of fostering collaboration within one's own institution.

Testing and Simulation: It May Be All Fun and Games until Someone Loses . . .

The pedagogical versus functional importance of information and communication technologies is often conflated for the simple reason that, despite the earlier chapters' emphasis upon the subsidiary role of technology in the creation of collaborative networked teaching and learning, the teaching goals are likely obstructed when there is a failure of a technology or an application. Such scenarios are avoided only when teachers have another means of communication with each other, a "Plan B," and/or the ability to creatively adapt alternatives on the fly. Here are a few examples of what has happened in collaborative networked sessions when someone loses a . . .

. . . a Visual Connection

Face-to-face connections are among the most effective tools for social learning made available by today's online technologies. There are myriad ways and means of establishing a real-time, face-to-face connection among learners in two geographically separated classrooms. That effectiveness is diminished in proportion to the clarity of the image, however.

A collaborative networked session that was planned to last seventy-five minutes ended only after twenty-two minutes because of the physical arrangement in one of the classrooms. None of this was expected or anticipated. The collaborating teachers had planned to use Skype in order to conduct a session where students had prepared brief statements and brought illustrative objects to show across the connection. TeacherA was in a rectangular classroom with a wall of outside-facing windows. Aimed at a roll-down screen on one of the "short walls" was a ceiling-mounted LCD projector. The screen itself was small, roughly five by seven feet. TeacherA had mounted a Web camera onto the edge of the screen.

There was very little collaboration possible when the networked session began. Streaming over to the other class was an "image" of TeacherA's classroom that resembled visions described by persons with near-death experiences. It was all bright light. TeacherA attempted to resolve the situation by pulling down the blinds. The resulting image streamed from the classroom was a pitch-black background pierced in one corner by the light from the ceiling-mounted LCD projector. When TeacherA turned on the fluorescent lights in the room, they flooded out the image of the other classroom on the wall-mounted screen. The situation was entirely unexpected, and everyone was quite frustrated with the "damned if you do, damned if you don't" nature of the lighting.

... an Audio Connection

Being heard by someone who can respond in real time is almost as powerful as face-to-face connections. Indeed, the effect may be even more powerful when teachers have collaborated to plan specifically for an audio-only connection.

A classroom in Canada was to be connected with one in Botswana. Prior testing had revealed that there was a difficulty obtaining sufficient bandwidth for a face-to-face connection, and so the plan was to simply use a Voice-over-Internet-Protocol (VoIP) connection. The collaborating teachers had decided against using a telephone connection because of the costs and bureaucratic difficulties involved with making international long-distance calls. All of these arrangements had been made between the offices of the collaborating teachers. They had never thought to test the connection between their actual classrooms.

On the day of the class session, both teachers set up their computers in their respective classrooms. As this was a VoIP connection, they had planned on simply plugging the Web cameras from their offices into the classroom computers. The first difficulty encountered seemed like a simple problem: drivers needed to be installed on the classroom computers to run the Web cameras. The bandwidth that limited the visual connection also affected the speed of the driver downloads, however. After a delay, the drivers were installed and the connection was initiated. What happened next was unexpected. The VoIP connection "went fuzzy" after roughly five minutes, and then degraded to become unrecognizable within seven minutes. The teachers had planned for a structured question-and-answer session, but the flow was fractured by the need to "hang up" and "redial" every five minutes. It became clear that the fractured nature of the session was taking a toll on student engagement, too. The session continued to its close, but the teachers agreed to make the exchange into an asynchronous exchange on their shared Moodle classroom forum.

... Network Bandwidth

The long-term impact of collaborative learning is established when teachers structure in-class activities whereby learners collaborative to create products and outcomes together. The functionality of most online applications used for collaborative networked sessions require some kind of consistent level of access to their networks. Restrictions or losses of network bandwidth may lead to disrupted connections and other gaps in service. These are not productive disruptions. Disengagement may begin, since learners may begin to assume that their partners are not unable to respond, but are unwilling to do so.

TeacherQ had planned with her collaborator for their classes to work together online to create responses to case studies being discussed during a face-to-face connection. They were using a videoconferencing unit to facilitate the face-to-face connection. The two classes were in very different kinds of classrooms, however. TeacherQ's class was in a Wi-Fi-equipped room, whereas the other class was in a hard-wired computer lab. To overcome the lack of computers in her room, TeacherQ planned to bring in a few dozen laptops to access the Wi-Fi network.

On the day of the collaborative networked learning session, everything went just as planned. That is, until the latter half of the session, when TeacherQ's class tried to access the online platform to create their shared responses. After passwords were entered and the collaborative platform was entered, hands began to shoot up in TeacherQ's classroom. Nearly everyone in the room began experiencing delays between their input of data and its appearance on their shared documents. Some began to be dropped out of the shared documents altogether. In the other classroom, the conclusion was inadvertently being drawn that TeacherQ's class had nothing to say. Perhaps they had not done their preparatory homework or not listened in class? TeacherQ used the videoconference unit to explain the difficulties in the room, and the agreement was to delay the collaborative response activity until the next class. TeacherQ would resolve the issue with her IT staff contact in the meantime.

What Happened?

In each of the above scenarios, the collaborating teachers arranged for a debriefing meeting shortly after their in-class collaborative networked session. The conclusion in each of these cases was that insufficient and inadequate testing led to a technology failure. For all involved parties, the technology failure introduced undue difficulty, stress, frustration, communication gaps, and learner disengagement. The importance of testing is not to be underestimated, as is the importance of doing tests that simulate the conditions under which the collaborative networked session will be conducted.

None of the collaborating teachers in these three scenarios were using a communications backchannel. To varying degrees, one teacher did not entirely know or understand the challenges faced by a partner. The scenarios are not exhaustive representations of what could possibly present a difficulty to a collaborative networked session. In the past, there have been more complex problems such as power outages in buildings and construction workers severing an institution's main network connection. All too often, the difficulties are relatively small in nature but large in effect, such as an unplugged cable or a missed software update. In all of these situations, the importance of a communications backchannel between teachers cannot be underestimated.

What Should Have Happened?

Create a Functional Simulation of Each Collaborative Networked Activity

Testing and simulation is the important, missing detail. The "rule of threes" guideline discussed in chapter 3 applies here, insofar as comprehensive testing is a part of the preparation phase. There are several layers of preparedness that must be established for an effective social learning plan to come into effect with collaborative networked learning sessions. All of them are a function of teacher preparation, such as preparing the learners and simulating the teaching and learning conditions for any test. Depending upon those conditions, the simulation checklist understandably alters and adapts. For example, here are some basic points to cover for functional simulations:

- *Check for software updates.* Even if an application is Web-hosted, it may require updated software. Any application using Adobe Flash and Apple QuickTime are prime examples, and applications such as Skype regularly require updates. A larger number of Web-based apps require the installation of apps or widgets into browsers, too.
- *Create accounts and share usernames.* Be it a teacher or a learner, everyone participating in a collaborative networked session that involves an online application likely must set up an account and communicate some details to whomever is organizing the activity. Otherwise, valuable time will be lost doing this during the session itself.
- *Mock accounts.* Teachers should establish "fake" accounts on the applications being used, and then test them from whatever devices might be used in the actual session. These mock accounts are also essential when testing the functionality of applications that will host multiple users.

During one simulation, a difficulty was discovered that required revising the entire activity. An online poll and spreadsheet was created with the intention of having the classes complete the survey and manipulate the data during a presentation shared by the collaborating teachers. The teachers created the poll and spreadsheet using their desktop computers, and one teacher tested both using an Android smartphone. During the simulation test the other teacher tried using an iPad, only to discover that the spreadsheet was completely inaccessible on iOS devices. Thankfully, these teachers were able to find an application and format that was "device agnostic" within the twenty-four hours prior to the actual collaborative networked class session.

What to Look Out For in the Simulation

While performing the simulation of each collaborative networked activity, each "side" of the connection should compile a document that records the exact conditions and results for each activity simulated. That document should be sure to pay attention to the following issues:

- Test all proposed connections using the actual planned devices in the actual rooms for the session. It may be useful to arrange the test with IT staff present. Be sure to give at least one week's notice for this kind of request.
- Be sure to follow all the steps in the detailed session plan in the correct succession of activities.
- Follow any of the exact instructions circulated to the classes. Do the instructions "work" when literally followed by someone new to the activity?
- To reiterate the first point: test all technology at the actual locations of the collaborative networked session. This includes whatever technology the class members may be expected to bring.
- Attempt to simulate the number of users supported by the devices and applications. Do they *really* work?
- Determine whether the technology and platforms are being pushed to their limits. Can either location trigger a failure? If so, precisely determine the point in conditions at which the failure occurs. This limit can then be noticed and hopefully avoided.
- Decide upon a backchannel mode for private teacher-to-teacher communications, and then test whether it works in both actual locations.
- Test all audio and visual equipment in their planned positions on location. Paying attention to such issues as video backlighting, audio feedback (that horrible screeching sound!), and viewing positions within the class.
- Establish the times required for setting up and taking down equipment. Always keep in mind that there might be conversations and questions fielded by teachers during these processes. And so, having a clear plan and understanding about this is very important.

Extend the Innovation 6.1

G. Brooke Lester

During a faculty-meeting discussion about assessment rubrics, a colleague asked, "But what keeps a rubric from being just another checklist?" As it happens, I had recently not only been revisiting Richard Feynman's participation in the Rogers Commission investigating the tragic Space Shuttle Challenger disaster, but had watched the movie *Apollo 13* with my son.

"Just another checklist"? The dismissive attitude implied toward "a checklist" brought me up short. Granted that any given checklist might be a good one or a bad one, and that the astronaut seated above a couple of million pounds of fuel hopes that the checklist at hand is a good one, I don't think you could find anyone involved in the launch sequence who thinks of that list dismissively as "just another checklist."

Loewen's bullet lists offer a template for the checklists that *you'll* be grateful for, perched as you are atop a couple of millions pounds of investment and expectations. If your Instructional Technology team does not yet offer a checklist for whatever regularly enacted digital-learning operations that faculty undertake, talk to someone on that team. Chances are that the checklist exists, if only in someone's head or circulated among IT staff. Get involved until it's a shared, openly available, faculty-IT commodity.

What If There Are Problems During the Simulation?

As already mentioned, the simulation and testing of technology is best done alongside IT staff. Of course, it should be underlined that there are limitations to IT staff and resources at institutions. IT staff likely need more than a week's notice to balance all their priorities with your request. It may be the case that some institutions have offices or personnel dedicated to helping teachers use technology in their classrooms. This would be the time to access such amazing resources.

After the simulation, several items should be attended to:

- What should be done if a difficulty is identified? The obvious options are either to revise the plan of activities or to troubleshoot the difficulty in question.
- Are there any updates that need to be requested from IT?
- What is the timeline for making any modifications and/or adjustments? And do these involve IT staff?

What If New Problems Arise During the Collaborative Networked Session?

Planning and simulating all the collaborative networked session activities does not necessarily mean that there will be no technical challenges during the actual session. New issues may arise that are completely unanticipated.

For example, there was a gold-medal game in the Olympics taking place precisely during a planned-for collaborative networked session. On one end of the connection, there was a complete loss of bandwidth because the college had decided to live-stream the event throughout the campus. At the other end, avid sports fans in the class were "multitasking" and losing engagement in the session. The teachers used a backchannel to communicate via text messaging, and decided two things: they would switch to chat-only communications among the groups in their classes, and they would project the game onto their large, main screens. Their activity continued without a hitch to the end of the class session.

In another example, teachers in a collaborative networked session planned to use Google Hangouts to facilitate face-to-face communications between the classes. At the beginning of the session, it quickly became apparent that, in one class, the browsers on their classroom computers did not have the Google Hangout plug-in installed. This meant that each computer needed to have someone access, download, and install the plug-in. There was no way that the teacher, alone, could do this in the space of the class session. And so she frankly asked her class to help each other solve the problem. The unexpected outcome was that learners from each class began using online chats to help each other install the plug-in, and then conduct unstructured sharing. The effect was to have the difficulty resolved while establishing collaborative problem solving!

From this experience come several important points about dealing with technical issues in class:

- Avoid panic when learners meet technical difficulties. Get them working on a task, and then focus on those who need more help.
- Have sufficient familiarity with the technologies used in order to assist other individuals.
- Realize that the class may have learners with sufficient technical knowledge to troubleshoot and support others in the room.

Follow-Up to a Collaborative Networked Teaching and Learning Session

History Needs Writing

Conducting a collaborative networked session is exhilarating and sometimes exhausting. With all the preparation and planning, there is much relief experienced when the plans are actualized and the session is enacted. Sometimes, when there are technical glitches, there is the added excitement of having overcome a challenge or problem. More often than not, there are unexpected flashes of insight or unique moments that take place among teachers and learners. People walk away from these experiences feeling as though something special just happened.

Because of these effects, the unique learning experience of collaborative networked teaching and learning needs to be written up into some kind of reflection. If teachers plan to conduct a series or succession of collaborations, then they clearly benefit from reflecting on their practice. Even if teachers do not plan to conduct another session, there is clearly a great worth in finding out what made the experience unique. The opportunities for insight that emerge from conducting a class session that is out of the ordinary may be useful in future, "ordinary" class sessions.

Teaching is a practice, therefore it is never perfect. The profession of teaching is one of constant learning. Reflecting on the collaborative networked session opens avenues for professional development, largely because the debriefing of networked sessions can be done collaboratively. Cross-institutional pedagogical reflection benefits from being low stakes, as it is outside the typical context for professional development.

Reflecting on the sessions should take place in stages:

- Individually:
  - *As soon as possible*—To take stock of the raw experience of the session, each teacher should find at least fifteen to thirty minutes to jot down some unstructured reflections. If this cannot be done immediately after the session, then these off-the-cuff reflections should be done within the first twenty-four hours.
  - *Within a few days*—The debriefing document mentioned below is a useful tool for moving beyond the raw experience to a metacognitive consideration of what actually happened.
- As collaborators:
  - *Within one week*—There should be an agreed-upon date during which a face-to-face debriefing discussion may take place. Usually, teachers find important differences and affinities by comparing notes on the "raw" experience as well as the more formal debriefing document.

Moving from individual to collaborative reflection is something that is often assigned by teachers, but not necessarily taken up as a professional practice. The best ideas for adjustments of planning may come from processing the similarities and differences in perspectives on the session. Furthermore, doing these reflections can lead to flashes of insight and creativity to support important developments in planning future learning experiences.

How to Debrief

There are two purposes for debriefing: one is to find out how to support effective teaching and learning, and another is to gather technical information efficiently to enable the efficient application of information and communication technologies in a learning environment.

Debriefing works through three questions:

- What happened?
- What are the implications?
- What are the applications?

A debriefing worth its salt is one that takes all possible perspectives into account. From police officers to parents to politicians to anyone who has played the children's game "telephone," the familiar experience is that everyone tells their story differently. Even more so is this the case when two geographically separated classrooms are taking part in an online learning experience. Take the number of stakeholders involved, from IT staff through to the learners in the class, and here are literally as many sides to the story of what "actually" takes place in a collaborative networked session. Whenever there are differences of perspective in teaching and learning, there are important pedagogical lessons and outcomes to be discovered.

Therefore, the answer to the question "What happened?" is really the question of "What was happening?" There is a lot going on in any class session, let alone a collaborative session. The objective is not to establish a unified narrative. Instead, both teachers should work to describe their own personal narratives of what happened. These should be as thorough as possible, because the teachers are the ones most invested in the outcomes of the session. As much as possible, the collaborating teachers should seek out opinions and perspectives from others, too. Precisely because of their differing experiences, the point of view from one learner to the next will be as different from theirs as the experience of any IT technician who was involved in the planning or production of the session.

By collating the collected viewpoints of all involved, the teachers can then start comparing notes to find out all the possible upshots and outcomes. And then, "What are the implications?" may start to be addressed. The comparison of perspectives will allow for the learning outcomes to be framed in qualitative terms. Teachers and learners often have differing opinions as to whether a class session has met its learning goal(s) and overall learning objective(s). By obtaining a clear sense of what happened, teachers may begin drawing conclusions about what learners discovered and processed in the running of the collaborative networked session. These qualitative observations will need to be conjoined with evaluations of the productions or evaluations related to the session.

Furthermore, the narratives of what happened will enable a discussion of what went well, and what could be better. Taking a positive approach to highlighting the successful aspects of a session will enable a lighter approach to the difficulties that may have been encountered. Sometimes one teacher will feel very successful, and the other will feel like a failure. A good teaching team is one capable of lifting each other's spirits. By framing the session in terms of what could be better, there is an application to all the activities in the session, even the most successful ones.

On more than one occasion, collaborating teachers have had completely different impressions of a particular activity's success within a networked session. In one case, there was a "discussion of the whole" that was thought to be a resounding success in one classroom and a complete failure in the other. Only when the teachers were discussing their narratives of the session activities was the difference revealed. Because they were conducting their debriefing session over a face-to-face connection, each could see the difference on the face of the other: one was smiling broadly and the other was sighing with exhaustion. They investigated the activity, and found two things: one class group was three times fewer in number than the other, and that class's teacher had his back to the Web camera. As a result, the large class became disengaged and distracted. The possibility that each teacher can have a completely different experience of an activity should lead to the consideration of the same for the learners in the classroom. Whenever possible, then, "classroom assessment techniques" should be used to gather learners' impressions.

There are other ways of asking "What are the implications?" These are questions about each collaborator's own knowledge and skills vis-à-vis collaborative networked teaching and learning. It is important to challenge each other in the following ways:

- What happened in this session that helped me know more about teaching in this context?
- What helped me obtain a better sense about what I already knew?
- What did I find out about teaching and/or learning from a new angle or perspective?
- What new directions or actions may I take in future teaching situations?

After moving through the first two questions, collaborating teachers may then more capably answer "What are the applications?" This is a question about making adjustments in current or future teaching plans. A useful debriefing is one in which all participants find opportunities to fine tune or revise their teaching. The discussions may help to articulate how the collaborative networked session addressed the classes' acquisition of skills or knowledge towards accomplishing the learning goals. Or, with the retrospect of debriefing, it may be possible to realize the need for adjusting either the goals or aspects of evaluation related to the learners' outcomes or productions.

In the longer term, the debriefing is useful to help adjust future collaborative networked teaching and learning sessions. Discoveries are often made on the ground about the limits or capabilities of technologies, programs, and applications. For example, one pair of collaborating teachers attempted to have their classes co-create posters using Prezi, which is an online "zooming" presentation tool. When used by individuals, this tool can make compelling presentations. Only in discussions with their learners did the teachers realize a major difficulty: people could see what others were doing, but could not communicate with them in real time (aside from writing actual text on the Prezi). During their debriefing, in between successive collaborative networked class sessions, the teachers devised a workaround. They asked their learners to switch over to a Google Presentation, which is slide-oriented presentation platform that has a built-in live chat function (as do all of the Google platforms: Document, Presentation, Spreadsheet, Drawing). The only the requirement was that their final creation consist of only one slide. The change in platform between class sessions made it possible for everyone to complete their projects. Such successful adjustments are usually only possible in the context of effective debriefing by the collaborating teachers.

The Debriefing Template

Below, on page 137, is a suggested format for a debriefing process. This particular debriefing template was developed in an actual collaborative networked teaching and learning context that involved over thirty teachers across several institutions and thousands of miles. As soon as their in-class collaborative sessions were done, each member of the teaching team independently completed the document and uploaded their version to a cloud-based file-sharing service. During the following week, the collaborators then arranged to compare and learn from each other in a real-time discussion.

It is very easy to create a similar document by inserting tables onto a blank word-processing file. For the purposes of collaborative discussion, the document can be created on a cloud-based application such as Google Docs or Microsoft 365 or Zoho Docs. The discussion of each partner's debriefing works best when the documents are made available to each other on a cloud-based file sharing service and when the discussion is conducted via a face-to-face communication application.

Part A of the document works through the first the two debriefing questions: What happened? What are the implications? Part B works through the third debriefing question: What are the applications? The most important application issue, from a pedagogical point of view, is to work through the accomplishment of the learning goals. Insights can be gained from reflection on learning goals, whether or not they were accomplished. Sometimes teachers are surprised when all the learning goals are accomplished. This can press the question of whether "the bar" was set too low, or whether there were highly effective activities whose structure lead to their efficient accomplishment. A thorough consideration of each and every learning goal articulated—those that are discipline specific as well as those that are transversal—is useful in these debriefings. Likewise, determining whether a sufficient level of collaboration was achieved is a question that each teaching team must decide upon together.

Paying attention to the construction of the debriefing document and agreeing upon the debriefing process is something clearly best done during the planning process, rather than just before or after the actual collaborative networked session. Doing so will help create focus on what teaching teams are looking for in their own quest for pedagogical effectiveness and professional development.

Collaborative Networked Teaching Debriefing Template

Part A: The Basics

1. What happened? Sketch the events of the class session in narrative or point form.

[ ]

2. What went well? Enter your descriptions into the table. Enter as many items as you wish by simply adding more rows. (Right-click and select "add rows below.")

Description:	Why was this the case?

3. What did not go well? Enter your descriptions into the table. Enter as many items as you wish by simply adding more rows. (Right-click and select "add rows below.")

Description:	Why was this the case?

4. What could be better? Any description in 1 or 2 has potential for improvement, either before, during or after the session. (Remember to add more rows: right-click and select "add rows below.")

Before the session?	During the session?	After the session?

Part B: Deepen your reflections
Be sure to complete this section individually prior to your real-time discussion.
You will reveal important insights about your collaboration!

a. Learning goals:

List each learning goal for your session:	Achieved? Yes/No	Why was this the case?

b. Communication and collaboration:

What examples of learner communication and/or collaboration took place during the session?	In your class OR with your partner's?	Why was this the case?

c. Technology:		
Itemize each technology used	Was it helpful? Yes/No	Why was this the case?

d. Assignments/homework linked to the session				
Assignment/ homework	Before, in, or after session?	<u>In</u> your class OR <u>with</u> your partner's?	Helpful? Yes/No	Why was this the case?

An example of a useful debriefing document.

The Final Detail: Fostering Stakeholders' Interest and Participation

The Benefits for Learners and Their Classes

Informed consent is important for full participation in collaborative networked teaching and learning. Classes must be informed as soon as possible about whether such a learning experience is forthcoming. It should never be a surprise, since this will have a negative impact on learner engagement and the contribution of the session to a course's overall learning objectives. For these reasons, there should be mention and discussion of plans for a collaborative networked session early in the term.

At the beginning of a term, most classes give their teachers the benefit of the doubt: whatever is listed in the course content on the first day of class is there on good faith. There is no guarantee that this optimism prevails throughout the term. Collaborative networked teaching and learning is not usually among the normal experiences of in-class sessions. Any sort of experimental activity needs an explanation, otherwise the running assumption will be that the session is an anomaly and it should be treated as such.

Therefore, not only should the design of a collaborative networked session be integrated with each teachers' course learning objectives, but there should also be clearly definable links to other content in the course, course assignments, and course evaluations. As one teacher noted, "I have to do PR before these sessions." These links need to be explained early on in the term, and they must be affirmed in all three phases of preparation, the actual session, and the debriefing. Doing so will validate the actual in-class collaborative networked session as well as validate the modeling of pedagogical experimentation. If teachers can make clear to their classes what are the direct connections to their learning and grades, then it should be possible to provide that explanation to any other stakeholder in their institutions.

Extend the Innovation 6.2

G. Brooke Lester

"Sometimes you eat the bear. Other times, the bear eats you." Loewen's experience provides a partial recipe for eating the bear: communicate overtly with your learners the straight line between the digital learning baked into the course design and their ability to engage the course's "big ideas," along with the performances by which they are to demonstrate particular enduring understandings.

Then there was the time the bear ate me. On the first evening of a new semester, at a school I only taught for occasionally, I chatted with some of the front-row learners while waiting for the top of the hour to arrive and class to begin. They had observed that I would be teaching the course online the following semester, and I remarked casually that some of the online collaborative projects that we'd be doing in this face-to-face class would also find a place in that later online class.

Oops. From that point, the narrative took shape among nervous learners that I was "using" them to prepare for my later online class, that this section was an "experiment." The prepared case that I would go on to make about learning goals (now decidedly on the defensive) fell on deafened ears. I had poisoned my own well with a casual remark before taking to my "prepared script." The next twelve weeks were an exhausting battle of inches.

The lesson for me? First: even the first session is too late (better to rouse interest in the precourse syllabus and emails). And second: after having worked up your "elevator speech" on why you do what you do, don't lose the moment by improvising before the curtain goes up. *Start on message and stay on message.*

The Benefits for Institutions

The success of any social-learning initiative depends upon its sustainability, and the sustainability of such projects rests upon the interest and participation of stakeholders throughout an institution. The benefits for teachers and students listed in chapter 1 above also apply to entire institutions. The competencies fostered by collaboration can be applied vertically and horizontally throughout a college's structure. Indeed, one of the surprising outcomes reported by teachers involved in successful collaborative networked teaching and learning projects is that they establish or improve their relationships with personnel throughout their institutions. By effectively communicating these benefits to stakeholders, and college administrators in particular, a collaborative networked teaching and learning initiative gains the support needed to start up as well as to continue over a longer term.

More specifically, there is a predictable range of "transversal connections" across units and departments that can be expected as benefits due to a collaborative networked teaching and learning project. In the world of IT and Internet security, transversal connections help bring together networks that would otherwise be unable to exchange data with each other. All sorts of security measures block these kinds of communications (e.g., encryption, authentication, firewalls, antivirus). In an analogous way, relationships among units and departments within an institution are often prevented by communication blockages. For example, there are usually administrative "buffers" that prevent IT staff from speaking to teachers, and teachers rarely speak with room scheduling or registrars. The positive impact of collaborative networked teaching and learning projects is that they effectively bring these people and their units into contact with each other.

- IT staff gain insights into instructional design.
- Teachers understand the actual work of IT staff.
- Administrative officers discover a direct connection to teaching and learning.
- A community of teaching and learning practice may emerge among teachers, staff, and administrators.

The overall benefit for institutions from collaborative networked projects is the emergence of an alignment between the goings-on of the classroom to the institutional mission or goals. The effect of these transversal connections leads to the cultivation of cross-cutting knowledge about procedures and workflows among the various units of the institution. Indeed, some new learner-centered discoveries about modification or enhancement of policies and procedures may emerge from these connections. One college, for example, was able to revitalize its direction for a classroom-redesign initiative. Within months, a wide consensus emerged for the initiative emerged from among the now-existing conversations among teachers, IT staff, facilities managers, and senior administrators. In other words, collaborative networked teaching and learning projects not only facilitate cooperation between separate institutions, but also within the institutions themselves.

Discussions with Administrators

The surest path toward initial and longer-term success for collaborative networked teaching and learning projects comes about by means of generating active interest by associate and faculty deans. Support from middle- and senior-level administrators brings about the possibility of sustaining a collaborative project over a series of academic terms, if not the normalization of the project into the ongoing operations of an institution. These persons are seen as the primary decision makers within the institution, and their support will guarantee the initial acceptance and compliance from other units in the institution.

There are several aspects of collaborative networked teaching and learning that may convince these leaders to find sufficient reason to advocate for a project within their institution. These points are in addition to the above discussion of transversal connections:

- Teachers' participation will cultivate their interest in professional development, since there is a clear connection between acquiring new teaching skills and introducing a new kind of learning experience to the classroom.
- Contextual learning may be brought into the classroom; this is effective as a stand-alone initiative, or as a means of preparation for service learning, internships, and mobility projects.
- The communication required among institutional units and/or departments may encourage and support innovations in workflows, communications, and the use of resources.
- Administrators' participation will provide a new avenue for relationships with other institutions; these relationships may take the form of a new partnership, a revived memorandum of understanding, an agreement to share resources, or even the possibility of an inter-institutional grant proposal.
- Collaborative networked teaching and learning projects foster expertise and capacities that support applications for development grants from governments, nongovernmental agencies, and private-sector interests.
- There are several connections for this kind of a project with an institution's strategic plan and/or vision. For example, connections can be drawn to objectives for community outreach, internationalization, regional outreach, online learning, pedagogical innovation, and enrollment strategies.

Embarking on a discussion such as this will almost immediately precipitate two questions from any smart administrator: What will this cost? What will I need to arrange? The first question should be answered in the context of experimentation, expansion, and normalization phases. There are different kinds of reasonable investments and accommodations to make in these phases. The costs for experimentation may range from next to nothing to the investment of teaching release for development. A motivated teacher may wish to experiment on a small scale, with the agreement to report back on the possibility of investment in a larger project. The expansion and normalization phases almost always require some kind of investment of institutional resources and teaching release, if only because this may generate the "critical mass" that leads to a normalized collaborative networked teaching and learning program. The investments range from equipment purchases to the approval for use of staff resources. All of this depends upon the existing state of personnel and resources, which may range anywhere from zero IT resources to well-staffed and well-equipped educational technology resources.

The second question may be answered with more specificity than the first. There is a certain set of actions that needs administrative-level approval and support in order to facilitate an effective social-learning project. The first is that the administrator grant permissions for involvement in the project. Ideally, this includes directives to departments or faculties for the support of the project, where chairs or coordinators are specifically asked to attend to the project. This kind of direction is almost always essential where it comes to course listing, scheduling, and room assignments. Without this assistance, a collaborative networked project will rarely be able to succeed. While it is not always necessary to make changes to course listings, doing so should be considered. The mention of a collaborative networked teaching and learning component in a course listing will ensure there is some level of consent to participation from the class involved. If there is to be a synchronous element to the teaching collaboration, then there must be a coordination of scheduling. These arrangements must be made well ahead of time and in accordance with the partnered institutions' workflows. Finally, the room assignment is an important consideration with regard to Internet connections, access to technology, and audio-visual dynamics. For example, the project will face challenges in a room without both Wi-Fi and hard-wired Internet connections or that lacks proper lighting.

The administrative support also extends to the relationship with the institution where the other collaborating teacher is located. There should be every effort made to facilitate a formal liaison for communications between similarly positioned administrators. Not only will this be useful in the event of future partnership agreements or inter-institutional grant applications, but doing so also ensures that both "sides" of the collaboration have the same level of commitment. The potential for power differences is at least addressed, if not minimized, by having conversations among administrators. While there may always be variations in terms of how much support is given, for example in training or technology, at least there is a clear answer to the important question of basic support for the collaboration.

Discussions with Staff

There are two kinds of staff from whom direct support should be garnered for a collaborative networked teaching and learning project. The precise terminology for their positions will vary, as well as their precise locations within the institution, but these staff may be conceived of as the pedagogical advisors and the IT services staff. Each of these kinds of staff fulfills an important role in supporting the development of a collaborative networked teaching and learning project through the phases of experimentation, expansion, and normalization.

Pedagogical Advisors

These personnel go by different names in every institution. Their role is to provide input to faculty for the development of skills and expertise in teaching and learning. They may also provide some level of advising with the use of technology for teaching and learning, too. Whatever the case, their purpose is to establish teaching excellence in an institution, and their job descriptions often involve reporting and documenting their efforts to bring about such results. A collaborative networked teaching and learning project may provide a new and highly interesting avenue for these persons to fulfill their institutional mission, and so their enthusiastic support is usually predictable.

What may a pedagogical advisor be able to do? One important function is advocacy. This staffperson may be helpful in establishing a liaison with more senior administrators, as well as with establishing support through other levels or units of the institution. It is likely that the pedagogical advisor has already met with the chairs and/or coordinators of an institution. Just as important, the pedagogical advisor may already have a relationship with the IT services personnel, and can both facilitate and advocate for the project. Furthermore, there is likely a similar person or staff unit at the collaborating teacher's institution. With communication between these functions of each institution, a greater degree of advocacy may be established. This would be of particular usefulness in the event of a partnership agreement or inter-institutional grant application.

There are many practical benefits to having the participation and support of pedagogical advisors, too. Their professional skills and knowledge may be drawn upon at many points throughout the iterative design process. Pedagogical advisors are usually trained in course design, and often have experience in doing consultations for educational technologies. Most often, there is much to be gained from inviting pedagogical advisors to accompany the experimental sessions for collaborative networked teaching and learning. Doing so provides them with an opportunity to understand more clearly just what is happening and how their skills may be of help. An extra set of hands and eyes comes in handy in the normal course of an experimental session, and is appreciated in the event of a difficulty or technical glitch. Furthermore, they may have observations that sharpen the effectiveness of future sessions.

IT Services Personnel

At the moment where collaborative networked teaching and learning makes use of information and communications technologies, the IT services personnel become important. When a teacher establishes positive and productive relationships with this unit, the implementation of technology in the classroom becomes so much easier. To establish such relationships, special care should be taken to note the consideration for IT personnel's unit role within educational institutions today. In perhaps no other unit is there as much demand for immediate service, sustained support, and responsiveness to new circumstances. IT services units often find themselves working in last-minute situations to support existing services or to implement the newest or latest decision made by senior administrators. With this in mind, it is useful for teachers to make requests for support well ahead of time. This kind of respectful etiquette can carry an initiative through circumstances that would otherwise cause failure for a collaborative networked teaching and learning project.

What may IT services personnel be able to do? They cannot magically solve every problem, but they certainly can provide training in aspects of technology that are not necessarily the domain of the pedagogical advisors. They can provide some layperson's explanations of technologies, or even provide a means of increasing technological literacy. Where they are essential is for communications with the

IT personnel of the partner institution. Putting them into conversation with each other is paramount to having a successful collaboration. Of course, there should always be a specific question or task to guide the communication. This could be as simple as having technicians test a VoIP (e.g., Skype) connection between collaborator's classrooms. Teachers must accompany IT services personnel for these tests; this is of utmost importance, because teachers should be able to communicate what possible difficulties were faced and how the problems were resolved. There should always be consultation with IT services personnel if, at any point, there is the option of making purchases to support a project.

There Will Always Be "Details"

Since collaborative networked teaching and learning relies upon relationships and communications among persons, there is never a time when "the details" fade completely into the background. A collaborative endeavor always involves working with people to sustain awareness, advocacy, and support. Each academic term has the potential to bring new advantages and challenges to a collaborative project. A supportive IT staff member might take a sick leave, or a new dean may be hired, or a new collaborator may be sought out at a new institution. As mentioned in the introduction to this chapter, "the details" must be kept in mind at least one semester prior to the advent of a collaborative networked teaching and learning project.

These details require a series of communications among different units and levels of the participating institutions. In particular, the collaborating teachers are testing the technologies involved in their activities. This chapter has focused first on the details that directly involve the collaborators: ensuring that all the planned-for activities will work across the involved technologies and platforms, and that reflection and debriefing follows upon the collaborative networked session. Finally, the chapter considered the important details of fostering collaboration within one's own institution. The success of effective social learning depends upon collaboration not only with another teacher, but with administrators, pedagogical advisors, and IT services personnel.

Chapter Response I—G. Brooke Lester
Creating a Community of Practice

What you think you don't have time for: *Learning the technology.* What you actually don't have time for: *Other people.*

Meeting with them. Bringing them up to speed on what you're trying to do. Learning from them what it is that they're trying to do. Figuring out how you might, sensibly, bear one another's burdens. Everybody's day is full. It's hard for anybody even to know what anybody *does* all day.

Not long ago, an experienced high school teacher "shadowed" a pair of students, each on a separate day.[1] For this instructor, who by his own account makes students sit through his own whole class session most days, it was a revelation that students "literally [sit] down the entire day." It may seem ludicrous that the instructor, for years, couldn't generalize his own classroom practices to imagine a full day reflecting those same practices (okay, it's a bit ludicrous). But, instructors are busy. Super busy. *Crazy* busy. And when you're crazy busy, you're not glancing over into the next cubicle over, so to speak, to see what life is like on the other side. Which is why the "shadow" exercise, which can seem preposterously unnecessary, is a stroke of genius.

In 2005–2006, faculty members at Luther Seminary, in St. Paul, Minnesota, arranged to sit in on one another's classes. This was *extraordinarily difficult* to arrange (because everyone is, seriously, crazy busy), as they related at the resulting SBL/AAR Annual Meeting workshop and co-authored book.[2] But this is what it takes, if we are to know as much about our colleagues' practices as does any student who comes through on a degree program. If this is what it takes for *faculty members* to learn about what each other do in the classroom, how is IT supposed to know? How is the president, or the board of trustees? Not to mention what we're grinding away on, outside of the classroom, during the rest of the day (and the evening, and the weekend, and over breakfast . . .).

At my own institution, we have succeeded in getting several of our faculty members engaged in digitally mediated teaching, mostly in the form of fully online

---

1. Grant P. Wiggins, "A Veteran Teacher Turned Coach Shadows 2 Students for 2 Days—A Sobering Lesson Learned," http://grantwiggins.wordpress.com/2014/10/10/a-veteran-teacher-turned-coach-shadows-2-students-for-2-days-a-sobering-lesson-learned/.
2. Mary E. Hess and Stephen Brookfield, *Teaching Reflectively in Theological Contexts: Promises and Contradictions* (Malabar, FL: Krieger, 2008). The conference session was "Teaching Reflectively in Theological Contexts: A Panel Discussion among Theological Disciplines," panel discussion presented at the annual meetings of the Society of Biblical Literature and the American Academy of Religion, San Diego, November 19, 2007.

classes. Being ethical, responsible professionals who care deeply about the education and formation of their learners, they each reflect earnestly and actively about their practices and the results that they see. Being super busy (crazy busy!), they do most of this reflection individually. Far, far more challenging than getting our school into more digitally mediated learning has been carving out time and space for collaborative sharing and reflection on practices in digital pedagogy. And again, this is *just among faculty members*. Apart from building bridges with IT. With the administration. With the trustees. Everybody's day is full.

What kind of "relief" would be needed to kickstart a "shadow" program at my school, involving faculty, IT, and administrators? (Let's start with just these on-campus folks and save the trustees for another day.) Each participant would need to be relieved of two days' work, so that faculty could "shadow" an IT staffer on one day and an administrator on another (and so on). These days would have to involve real relief, not just putting work off until another day (crazy busy). Participants could submit which day of the week is likely best for them, and leader/shadow pairs could be drawn in part on this criterion. Faculty outnumber adminstrative and IT staff, but this fact can be managed. After all, not every faculty member would need to lead a shadow, as long as each IT staffer and adminstrator gets to shadow some instructor or other. It's true that IT staffers and adminstrators, being so outnumbered (at least where I am), would have the burden of leading a lot of shadows. Perhaps faculty shadows could double up on adminstrators and IT, so that these lead two faculty shadows on a given day.

What's important, as with the high school instructor who shadowed his students models well, is that the "shadow" is not simply an observer: she needs to shed her sense of looking in from the outside, and *be* one among those whom she shadows:

> My task was to do everything the student was supposed to do: if there was lecture or notes on the board, I copied them as fast I could into my notebook. If there was a Chemistry lab, I did it with my host student. If there was a test, I took it (I passed the Spanish one, but I am certain I failed the business one).

What will you "fail" as an IT staffer? As an administrator? What will everyone learn about the domains not their own? In Loewen's terms, what "community of teaching and learning practice may emerge among teachers, staff, and administrators"? Who knows what possibilities lurk in the hearts, minds, offices, and daybooks of all who spend their days supporting higher education? The Shadow knows.

Chapter Response II—*Christopher J. Duncanson-Hales*
Creating Communities of Scholars

In chapter 6, Loewen outlines some of the benefits of collaborative networked teaching and learning for a variety of stakeholders, including faculty, administration, students, and so forth. As important as getting the "buy-in" of our students is getting the administrative and other support of our colleagues.

Since beginning this project, I have experienced a bit of what I call the Ford Tempo effect. Let me explain: when I was in high school, when it came time for my family to obtain a new car, my dad chose a silver Ford Tempo. The car was nothing special; however, I thought it must be one of the most popular cars on the market. It had to be, because I started to see it everywhere. My dad suggested that it wasn't that the Tempo was any more popular than any other car but that our recent acquisition drew my attention to the model so that I noticed what in the past would go unnoticed.

Working with Lester and Loewen on this project has had a similar effect. As I've been reflecting and writing on this topic, I've begun to notice examples of collaborative and networked teaching where in the past they might have gone unnoticed. Indeed, one of the great gifts of Loewen's text is both to draw our attention to what is already being done while providing a framework to be more intentional about our pedagogical approach to these projects.

Two examples that come to mind which illustrate both the need for support and the challenges of colleague acceptance both recently occurred in my faculty. The first example involves my chair in the department of philosophy at the University of Sudbury. Over coffee one morning, I was discussing collaborative networked teaching and learning with one of my colleagues and a student. I told them of the great potential for collaborative networked teaching and learning at our institution, especially when our catchment area includes the remoter regions of northeastern Ontario.

My colleague's rather blasé reply was, "Oh, Paolo's been doing that for a couple of years now." Given the geographic context of my institution, I should not have been so surprised that others were experimenting with collaborative networked teaching and learning. Nevertheless, I was pleased to learn that my new department chair, Paolo, had been experimenting with collaborative networked teaching and learning, particularly in light of Loewen's advice for securing administrative support for collaborative networked teaching and learning,. Paolo's sessions, developed with a colleague at the University of Texas, involve the synchronous video presentations of introductory philosophy student's essays that had been shared prior to the session. When I spoke to Paolo about these sessions, he shared with me some of the challenges he had encountered, including technical limitations with bandwidth, student access to Skype subscriptions, and the like.

As we spoke, it became even more clear how valuable and, more importantly, practical this book will be to educators like myself and Paolo. In many respects, Paolo's represents a typical approach when we first embark on something that is perceived as new or innovative. Without past experiences to reference, we are forced to continually reinvent the wheel. The benefit of Loewen's approach is that, to borrow his analogy, it allows us to true the wheel rather than reinvent it.

The other example that comes to mind illustrates the value of collaborative networked teaching and learning to smaller institutions and programs. The University of Sudbury is a small, bilingual, liberal-arts institution that, according to the university profile "was founded as Collège du Sacré-Coeur in 1913. For many years it was the only institution of higher learning in Northern Ontario. In 1957, it changed its name and began to exercise its full teaching and degree-granting powers."[3]

One of the challenges facing the University of Sudbury, which is by no means unique to this institution, is declining enrollment in the liberal arts. This, in some respects, is exacerbated by the bilingual nature of the institution. One of the means the university is embarking on to preserve its bilingual offerings is to use networked teaching and learning to offer a course in philosophy for three institutions.

The pilot for this effort is being run in the winter term of 2015 and will involve one instructor located in Sudbury offering a course locally to students in Sudbury and synchronously to students at College Dominican and Saint Paul University in Ottawa, Ontario. What distinguishes this course from the collaborative networked teaching and learning Loewen proposes is that, rather than using technology to punch holes between classrooms, technology is being used to extend the Sudbury classroom to Ottawa. While not necessarily an ideal collaboration, it ought to provide interesting insights into the potential for collaborative networked teaching and learning. One can imagine smaller programs teaming up in this way to salvage low-enrollment courses whose intrinsic value goes beyond the extrinsic value of enrollment popularity. While the ethics of using this satellite approach for low-enrollment courses as a means to avoid new hires, whether tenure track or adjunct, at the remote site needs to be given careful consideration, some compromise is necessary if these low-enrollment courses and programs are to endure.

It is increasingly becoming evident that we are in the midst of a global shift in the theory and praxis of postsecondary education. This has created tremendous challenges for full-time faculty, precarious part-time faculty, administrators, and students alike. The great promises of the massive open online courses seem to have been overstated, suggesting that bigger is not always better. As our institutions continue to evolve, collaborative networked teaching and learning is one means by which we as educators can respond to the global realities of our world today. The advantage of this approach is that, by knocking a hole between classrooms, collaborative networked teaching and learning bridges the gap between the particularities of our local classrooms and the universality of postsecondary education in the era of globalization. In so doing, it provides one method for harnessing the promise of the digital ages by globally networking intimate, rather than massive, communities of scholars.

---

3. "Profile," University of Sudbury, http://usudbury.ca/index.php/en/university-of-sudbury/profile.

Selected Bibliography

Anderson, L.W., et al. *A Taxonomy for Learning, Teaching, and Assessing: A Revision of Bloom's Taxonomy of Educational Objectives.* New York: Longmans, 2001.

Bakhtin, Mikhail. "Toward a Methodology for the Human Sciences." In Caryl Emerson and Michael Holquist, eds., *Speech Genres and Other Late Essays*, 159–72. Trans. Vern W. McGee. Austin: University of Texas Press, 1986.

Bloom, B. S., et al. *Taxonomy of Educational Objectives: The Classification of Educational Goals.* Handbook I: Cognitive Domain. New York: Longmans, 1956.

Boule, Michelle. *Mob Rule Learning: Camps, Unconferences, and Trashing the Talking Head* Medford, NJ: CyberAge Books, 2011.

Boyer, Ernest L. *Scholarship Reconsidered: Priorities of the Professoriate.* San Fransisco: Jossey-Bass, 1997.

Carr, Nicholas. "The Hierarchy of Innovation." *Rough Type.* May 14, 2012. http://www.roughtype.com/?p=1603.

Cleese, John. "Lecture on Creativity." http://news.genius.com/John-cleese-lecture-on-creativity-annotated.

Coyle, Sharon, and Nathan Loewen. "Opening Up the Classroom: Why and How You Might Try a Bit of Virtual Team Teaching!" In T. Bastiaens & G. Marks, eds., *Proceedings of World Conference on E-Learning in Corporate, Government, Healthcare, and Higher Education 2012*, 97–101. Chesapeake, VA: AACE, 2013.

Davis, James R., and Bridget D. Arend. *Seven Ways of Learning: A Resource for More Purposeful, Effective, and Enjoyable College Teaching.* Sterling, VA: Stylus, 2013.

Derrida, Jacques. "Hostipitality." In Gil Anidjar, ed. and trans., *Acts of Religion*, 356–420. New York: Routledge, 2002.

Downes, Stephen. "What Connectivism Is." http://halfanhour.blogspot.co.uk/2007/02/what-connectivism-is.html.

———. "The MOOC Guide: CCK08—The Distributed Course." https://sites.google.com/site/themoocguide/3-cck08---the-distributed-course.

———. "A True History of the MOOC." http://www.downes.ca/presentation/300.

Drolet, Julie. "Getting Prepared for International Experiential Learning: An Ethical Imperative." In Rebecca Tiessen and Robert Lee Huish, eds., *Globetrotting or Global Citizenship?: Perils and Potential of International Experiential Learning*, 185–97. Toronto: University of Toronto Press, 2014.

Fink, L. Dee. *Creating Significant Learning Experiences: An Integrated Approach to Designing College Courses.* San Francisco: Jossey-Bass, 2003.

Gallagher, Edward J., and Stephen A. Tompkins. "Improving the Discussion Board." Lehigh University. August 2006. http://www.lehigh.edu/~indiscus/.

Glennon, Fred. "Promoting Freedom, Responsibility, and Learning in the Classroom: The Learning Covenant a Decade Later." *Teaching Theology and Religion* 11, no. 1 (2008): 32–41.

Gottwald, Norman K. "Framing Biblical Interpretation at New York Theological Seminary: A Student Self-Inventory on Biblical Hermeneutics." In Fernando F. Segovia and Mary Ann Tolbert, eds., *Reading from This Place, Vol. 1: Social Location and Biblical Interpretation in the United States*, 251–61. Minnneapolis: Fortress Press, 1995.

Graham, Mark. "Time Machines and Virtual Portals: The Spatialities of the Digital Divide." *Progress in Development Studies* 11, no. 3 (July 1, 2011): 211–27.
Hess, Mary E., and Stephen Brookfield. *Teaching Reflectively in Theological Contexts: Promises and Contradictions*. Malabar, FL: Krieger, 2008.
Höpken, Wolfgang. "Learning to Live Together: Fighting Stereotypes from Textbooks to the Internet." In Daniel Laqua and Aurore Salinas, eds., *New Ignorances, New Literacies: Learning to Live Together in a Globalizing World*, 138–44. Paris: UNESCO, 2005.
Hurtado, Sylvia, et al. *Undergraduate Teaching Faculty: The 2010–1011 Heri Faculty Survey*. Los Angeles: Higher Education Research Institute, 2012.
Jorgenson, Shelane, and Lynette Shultz. "Global Citizenship Education (GCE) in Post-Secondary Institutions: What Is Protected and What Is Hidden under the Umbrella of GCE?" *Journal of Global Citizenship & Equity Education* 2, no. 1 (Special Edition, 2012).
Learning Disabilities Association of Ontario. *Learning Disability Statistics*. http://www.ldao.ca/introduction-to-ldsadhd/ldsadhs-in-depth/articles/about-lds/learning-disabilities-statistics/.
Loewen, Nathan. "La Pédagogie interculturelle: favoriser l'internationalisation dans le cadre d'une pédagogie de la tolérance positive." *Pédagogie Collégiale* 26, no. 3 (Spring 2013): 29–34.
Marzano, Robert J. *A New Taxonomy of Educational Objectives*. 2d ed. Newbury Park, CA: Corwin, 2000.
McGuire, Joan M., Sally S. Scott, and Stan F. Shaw. "Universal Design for Instruction." *Remedial & Special Education* 24, no. 6 (November 2003): 369–79.
Noyd, Robert. "A Primer on Writing Effective Learning-Centered Course Goals." http://www.designlearning.org/wp-content/uploads/2010/03/Writing-Good-Learning-Goals-by-Robert-Noyd-US-Air-Force-Academy.pdf.
Palmer, Parker J. *The Courage to Teach: Exploring the Inner Landscape of a Teacher's Life*. 10th Anniversary Edition. San Fransisco: Jossey-Bass, 2007.
Rorabaugh, Pete, and Jesse Stommel. "Twitter Vs. Zombies: New Media Literacy & the Virtual Flash Mob." July 21, 2013. http://www.jessestommel.com/blog/files/twitter_vs_zombies.html.
Sahlins, Chris. *Gifts and Commodities*. London: Academic Press, 1982.
Siebdrat, Frank, Martin Hoegl, and Holger Ernst. "How to Manage Virtual Teams." *MITSloan Management Review*. http://sloanreview.mit.edu/article/how-to-manage-virtual-teams/.
Tiessen, Rebecca, and Robert Lee Huish, eds. *Globetrotting or Global Citizenship? Perils and Potential of International Experiential Learning*. Toronto: University of Toronto Press, 2014.
University of Guelph. "Universal Instructional Design Principles at the University of Guelph." N.d. http://www.uoguelph.ca/tss/uid/uidprinciples.cfm.
———. "Open Learning and Educational Support." N.d. http://www.coles.uoguelph.ca/default.aspx.
UNSECO. *Intercultural Competencies: Conceptual and Operational Framework*. Ed. Intersectoral Platform for a Culture of Peace and Non-Violence, Bureau of Strategic Planning. Fontenoy, France: UNESCO, 2013.
Wesch, Michael. "Context Collapse." July 31, 2008. http://mediatedcultures.net/youtube/context-collapse/.
Wiggins, Grant P. "A Veteran Teacher Turned Coach Shadows 2 Students for 2 Days—a Sobering Lesson Learned." http://grantwiggins.wordpress.com/2014/10/10/a-veteran-teacher-turned-coach-shadows-2-students-for-2-days-a-sobering-lesson-learned/.
———. and Jay McTighe. *Understanding by Design*. Exp. 2d ed. Alexandria, VA: Association for Supervision and Curriculum Development, 2005.
———. *Understandng by Design Professional Development Workbook*. Alexandria, VA: Association for Supervision and Curriculum Development, 2004.

www.ingramcontent.com/pod-product-compliance
Lightning Source LLC
Chambersburg PA
CBHW071208070526
44584CB00019B/2957